GUIDE TO 14 ASIATIC LANGUAGES

GUIDE TO 14 ASIATIC LANGUAGES

ANDREW BOYD

GYAN

Published by

GYAN

Gyan Publishing House
5, Ansari Road
Daryaganj, New Delhi-110002
Phone: 011-47034999, 9811692060
E-mail: books@gyanbooks.com

Distribution Network
gyanbooks.com
India, USA, Canada, UK, Australia, France

ISBN : 9788121244077 (PB)
First Published, London, 1947

2nd Impression 2020

Printed at: Gyan Press, Delhi.

Guide to 14 Asiatic Languages
Author: Andrew Boyd

GUIDE TO 14 ASIATIC LANGUAGES

by

ANDREW BOYD

LONDON
THE PILOT PRESS LTD
1947

CONTENTS

Foreword

I hope this handbook will smooth the path of some of the many English-speaking travellers who will, in the very near future, visit the newly awakened East. It is not a book for the pundit; in fact, I have tried to eliminate the high-flown language so dear to the Oriental grammarian, and so unhelpful to the traveller who is trying to make minor purchases in a small bazaar.

It may seem presumptuous to claim that one small book will be of real service as a guide to the thousand tongues of Asia. But it is surprising how far the dozen *linguæ francæ* of the East will serve the wanderer even in remote places. Arabic, Turkish and Persian between them will take him along all the shores, and through most of the interior, of the great region known as the Middle East, from North Africa to the frontiers of India. In India itself there are reckoned to be some two hundred languages and many more dialects; but the traveller is not likely to get into difficulty if he commands a few words of Hindustani (Urdu), Bengali and Tamil. Burmese, Siamese and Malay will serve most of his purposes in South East Asia, including the East Indies; the two forms of Chinese given in this book (Mandarin and Cantonese) will be of value not only in China, Manchuria and Formosa, but also in the countless centres of Chinese colonization between

Singapore and Manila; and Japanese too may be found useful in Korea and other places outside Japan proper, although it is fortunately no longer fashionable in Rangoon, Batavia or Shanghai. Finally, the increasing importance of the Soviet Union in Asiatic affairs prompts the inclusion of a vocabulary of Russian in this book. While Russian can in no sense be called an Asiatic tongue, no linguistic handbook for Asia would be complete if it omitted the language which dominates the northern half of the continent much as English dominates the southern littoral.

Asiatic languages are certainly no more difficult than European ones. Many, including Chinese, Siamese and Malay, possess a beautiful simplicity unmarred by any of the infuriating conjugations and declensions so prevalent in the West. Again the fact that stress is usually very even in an Asiatic language eliminates the bewildering business of 'swallowed' syllables, which often baffles the student of English—or, for that matter, of Russian. The absence of any equivalent for the English verb 'to have' may seem at first sight a deficiency in several of the languages included in this book; but at least it protects the beginner from the very natural but fatal error of inserting a dictionary translation of 'have' into idiomatic phrases intended to convey the English 'have you finished?' 'I have to go,' or 'he will have some made.' Where an equivalent for the basic meaning of 'have' exists, it is shown in the lists opposite 'possess'; where none exists the reader should refer to the notes at the end of each section. These notes do not profess to cover the grammars of the languages concerned; but it should be possible for the beginner to construct simple sentences with no more aid than they provide.

The 'Glossary' contained in Part 4 of this book is intended to help the newcomer to the East to understand the commonest of the many strange words which he will hear on the lips of other English speakers, and which belong to no local language. Some, like *toddy*, *godown*, or *mofussil* are corruptions, often unrecognizable, of Asiatic words; others, such as *chilli*, *dengue*, *peon*, and *tiffin*, were brought to the East by early Europeans, and are firmly established in Anglo-Asiatic speech.

Throughout the four years of residence in various parts of Asia during which I compiled this book, I received invaluable assistance from many people of many communities; my special thanks are due to Miss Y. P. Loke, Colonel Stanley Lemin, Major Frank H. Burden and Subedar Jarasindh Singh Bisht. I must, however, take full responsibility for any errors which the more vigilant and expert reader may detect; and I would be most grateful for corrections, amplifications or suggestions from any quarter.

ANDREW BOYD.

Rangoon, 1945.

STANDARD PRONUNCIATION

VOWELS:

a as in 'à la carte'

ai as 'eye'

au as 'ow' in 'now'

aw as in 'law'

e as in 'bed' (final e is never silent)

ey as in 'grey'

i as in 'machine'

o as in 'robe'

oi as in 'join'

ö as 'or' in 'work'

ụ as in 'rude'

ü as in German 'über'; as u in French 'du,' or ui in Scots 'guid'; a high sound almost resembling ee in 'keen'

' a swallowed sound or catch in the voice, as in 'that'll do,' 'h'm'

CONSONANTS:

b, d, f, j, k, l, m, n, p, t, v, w, x, z as normally in English

g as in 'gun'

h as in 'hard' (except in combinations ch, gh, kh, dh, th)

ch as in ' church '

kh as ch in Scots ' loch ' or German ' ach '

gh as in ' lough ' or ' ugh '

dh as ' th ' in ' clothing '

th as in ' cloth '

q as in ' quay ' or ' quoit '

r always sounded ; *sporn* would be pronounced like ' sporran,' not like ' spawn '

s as in ' say '

y as in ' you ' (except in combination ey, above)

Part One

TURKISH

ARABIC (WESTERN)

ARABIC (EASTERN)

PERSIAN

HINDUSTANI (URDU)

ENGLISH	TURKISH	ARABIC (W.)
above	yoqari	foq
absent	ghayib	ghayib
accident	hadise	hadis
address	khitab	khitab
after	badehu	ba'd
afternoon	ikindi	ba'd ed duhr
again	bir daha ; tekrar	saniyan
age	yash	'omr
alive	diri ; hayya	hai ; tayyib
all	hep ; külli	kull
all right	eyi ; vesselam	tayyib ; zen
allow	izin	azan ; samah
alone	tenha	wahdo
also	da ; dakhi	kaman
always	hemishe; dayima	daiman ; kull waqt
and	le ; ve	wa
angry	darghin	za'lan
animal	haivan	haiwan
ant	qarinja	nimla
anything	her hangi biri	ai she
are	dirlar	—
arm	bazu ; qol	silah
army	ordu ; leshker	geysh
around	etraf	haw'l
arrangement	tertib	tartib
arrive	väsül ol–	wasal
ask	sor–; istid'a	saal ; talab

ARABIC (E.)	PERSIAN	HINDUSTANI
foq	bala	–ke upar
ghayib	ghayeb	ghair hazir
musiba	hadese	hadisa
kateb	invan	pata
ba'd	ba'd az	–ke bad
ba'd ed duhr	ba'd ez zohr	sham
tekrar	baz ; dobare	phir b'i
'amr	senn	umr
hai ; tayyib	zande	zinda
kull	tamam	sab ; tamam
tayyib ; zen	khaili khub	ach'a ; ba'ut ach'a ; t'ik'e
semah ; rakhkhas	ijazat dih–	ijazat de–
wahdi	tanha	akela
ham ; aidhan	ham ; niz	b'i ; aur
daiman ; kull waqt	hamisha	hamesha
wa	va ; o	aur
za'lan	ghazabnak	khafa
haiwan	janivar	janwar
nimla	murcha	chiunti
she	har chiz	koi chiz
—	and	hain
qitf	bazu	bazu
jesh	lashkar ; artesh	fauj
haw'l	dor–i	–ke as pas
tadbir	tamyiz ; nezam	bandobast
wasal	ras–	pahunch–
saal ; talab	so'al kun– ; talab kun–	puch– ; mang–

ENGLISH	TURKISH	ARABIC (W.)
at	–de ; yan	'and
back (noun)	arqa ; geri	gafa ; dahr
bad	fena	battal ; sharir
bag	khurj ; kese	kis ; gonia
bandage	sarghi	rubat
barber	berber	mizeyyin
basket	seped	sell
bath (tub)	hamam	hamam
bathe	yuqa–	isthamma
bathroom	banyo	hamam
be	dur ; dir	—
beans	baqla ; fasulya	fasulya
beautiful	güzel	gamil
because	zira ; chünki	'ashan
become	lash–	shar
bed	yataq ; dösheg	farash
bedroom	yataq odasu	odet en nom
before (time)	evvel	qabl
begin	bashla–	ibtada
behind	ard	wara ; khalf
bell	chan ; chingirdaq	gar's
below	alt	taht
bench	sura	maq'ad
best	en eyi	el ahsan
between	ara	ben
big	böyük ; iri	kebir
bill (account)	hisab	hisab
bird	qush ; mürgh	ter
black	qara ; siyah ; esved	eswed

ARABIC (E.)	PERSIAN	HINDUSTANI
'and	dar ; tu ; ru	–ke pas ; –men
jafa ; dahr	pusht	pit'
sharir ; kharab	bad ; kharab	kh'rab
kis ; jonia	kise ; kif	bori
laffafa	laffafa	patti
mizeyyin	dallak	hajam ; nai
sell	sabad ; zanbil	tokri
hamam	hamam ; ghusl	ghusl
tahammam	ghusl kun–	ghusl kar–
hamam	ghusl khana	ghusl khana
—	hast	ho–
fasulya	lubiya	phali
latif ; hasan	ghashang	khubsurat
min sebeb	chun (ke)	kiunkih
shar	shau– ; bash–	hota ho–
farash	takht i khab	palang ; charpai
jubbat en nom	khab–gah	sone ka kamra
qabl	pish az	–se pa'le
abda	shuru kun–	shuru kar–
wara ; khalf	pusht–i	–ke piche
jur's	zang	ghanta
taht	pa'in	–ke niche
takhat	saku	chauki
el ahsan	bihtarin	sab se ach'a
ben	miyan–i	–ke darmian
kebir	buzurg	bara
hisab	hisab	hisab
ter	paranda ; murgh	chiria
eswed	siyah	kala

ENGLISH	TURKISH	ARABIC (W.)
blacksmith	demirji	haddad
blanket	yorghan	hiram
blood	qan ; dem	dem
blue	mavi ; lajiverd	azraq
board	tahta	loh
boat	qayiq ; filiqa	markeb
boil, to	qayna– ; pishir–	salaq
bone	kemik	'adma
book	kitab	kitab
boot	chizmey	gazma
born, to be	dogh–	itwalad
box	sandiq	sanduq
boy	oghlan ; chojug	walad
brass	pirinj	nahas
bread	ekmek ; pidey	'esh
break, to	qir–; kesr et	keser
bribe, a	rishvet	reshwa ; bartil
brick	tughla	tuba
bridge	köprü	kubri
brother	qardash ; birader	akh
brush, a	fircha	fursa
build	bina et– ; yap–	bena ; 'ammar
building, a	bina ; tamir	bina
bullock	tosun	tor
burn, to	yaq– ; ihraq et–	ahraq
bush	chali	gaba
business	umur ; ish	shughl
buy	satin al– ; ishtira et–	ishtara
by	–le	'and ; bi

ARABIC (E.)	PERSIAN	HINDUSTANI
haddad	ahenger	lohar
zuliya ; planket	jul ; patu	kambal
dem	khun	khun
azraq	abi	nila
loh	takht	takhta
markeb	qaiq ; kashti	kishti
fawwar	jush kun–	ubal–
'adma	ustukhan	haddi
kitab	kitab	kitab
qandara	putin	juta
mawlud	paida shan–	paida ho–
sanduq	sanduq ; jaba	sanduq ; bak's
walad	pisar	chokra ; larka
prinj	birinj	pitaĺ
'esh ; khubz	nan	roti
keser	shikan–	tut– ; tor–
reshwa ; bartil	rishva	rishwat
tabuqa	ajur	int
jisr	pul	pul
akh	baradar	b'ai
farrach	burush	bras
bena ; 'ammar	saz	bana–
bunyan	imarat	imarat
tor	gav	bail
ahraq	suz–	jala–
'uleq	butah	j'ari
shughl ; tajara	tejarat	kam ; bat
ishtara	khar–	kharid–
'and ; bi	ba ; az	–se ;–ke sat'

B

ENGLISH	TURKISH	ARABIC (W).
call (for)	chaghir–	nadah
camp	ordu	mi'askar
can (is able)	–bil–	aqdar
cannot	–ma–	ma aqdarsh
candle	mum ; sham	shema'
cane	qamish	'asaya
carpenter	dürger	naggar
carpet	hali ; kilim	busat
carriage	araba	'arabia
cart	qanli	'arabia karo
cat	kedi	qutta
catch, to	tut–	mesek
cave	maghara ; in	maghara
ceiling	tavan	saqf
chain	zenjir	salsil
chair	sandalya	kursi
change, to	deyish– ; boz–	beddel
check (bill)	hisab	hisab
chief	sheykh ; bash	rayyis ; sheykh
child	chojug	walad
choose	ikhtiyar et–	ikhtar
church	kilisey	kanisa
cigarette	zigaret	zigara
city	shehr	wilaya ; medina
clean	temiz	nedif
clerk	kyatib ; mamur	katib
climb	turman–	issa'bat
clock	sa'at	sa'a
cloth	bez	gukh
clothes	chuqa ; ruba	hidum
cloud	bulut	sahab

ARABIC (E.)	PERSIAN	HINDUSTANI
sah	sada kun–	bula–
mi'askar	urdu	parao
aqdar	tavan–	sak–
ma aqdarsh	na mi tavanad	na'in sak–
shema'	sham'	mom–batti
'asaya	ta'limi	bet
najjar	najjar	mistri
zulia	qali	dari
'arabia	kaliska	gari
'arabia karo	gari	gari
bazzuna	gurbah	billi
mesek	gir–	pakar–
maghara	ghar	ghar
saqf	saqf	ch'at
salsil	zanjir	zanjir
kursi	sandali	kursi
beddel	tabdil kun–	badli kar–
hisab	hisab	hisab
rais ; sheykh	ra'is	sardar ; khan
walad	bacha	bach'a
ikhtar	muntakhab kun–	ch'un–
kanisa	kalisa	girja
zigara	sigari	sigaret ; biri
wilaya ; medina	shahr	shahr
nedif	pak	saf
katib	mirza ; munshi	babu
issa'bat	bala rav–	char'–
sa'ad	sa'at	g'ari
kham ; chit	parcha	kapra ; sari
hudum	rakht ; libas	kapre
ghema	ab'r	badal

ENGLISH	TURKISH	ARABIC (W.)
coat	setri	sitra
cock	khoroz ; musluq	dik
coffee	qahva	qahwa
cold	sovuq ; nevazil	barid
collar	yaqa	yaqa
comb	taraq ; shaney	misht
come	gel–	ga
concerning	dayir	min gehet
cook, a	ashji	tabbakh
cook, to	pishir–	tabakh
corner	köshey ; bujaq	zawia
correct	doghrul	sahih
cost (noun)	qimet	qima
cotton	pamuq	qutn
count	sai– ; tadad et–	'add
country	memleket	memleka ; bilad
courtyard	havli	hosh
cover, to	ört–	ghatta
cow	inek	baqara
crowd	qalabaliq	zahma
cup	finjan	finjan
cupboard	dolab	dulab
curtain	perdey	sitara ; parda
cushion	yasdiq	mekhadda
cut, to	kes– ; qat et–	qata'
daily	günlük ; yevmi	yomi
damage	zarar ; saqatliq	darar
dance, to	raqs et–	raqass
danger	tehlikey ; mukhatara	khatar

ARABIC (E.)	PERSIAN	HINDUSTANI
sitra	kot	kot
dik	khurus	murgha
gahwa	qahva	qahva ; koffi
barid	sar'd	t'anda
yaqa	yaghey	kolla
misht	shaney	kangi
ja	a–	a–
min jehet	babat–i–	–ki babat
tabbakh	ash–paz	khansama ; bawarchi
tabakh	paz–	paka–
zawia	gusha	kona
sahih	durust	t'ik
qima	qimat	qimat
qutn	pembey	rui
'add	shumar–	gin–
memleka ; bilad	mulk	mulk
hosh	medan	angan
ghatta	pushi–	d'ak–
baqara ; hasha	gav–i madah	gae
izdaham ; jama'a	izdiham	b'ir
finjan ; piala	finjan ; piyala	piala
dulab	almari	almira
parda	pardah	parda
mekhadda	balish	gaddi
qata' ; jass	bur–	kata–
yomi	har ruz	rozana ; roz roz
darar	khesarat	nuqsan
raqass	raghsi–	nach–
khatar	khatar	khatra

ENGLISH	TURKISH	ARABIC (W.)
dark	qaranliq ; zulmet	mi'attim
date (day)	tarikh	tarikh
daughter	bint ; dükhtür	bint
dawn	fejr ; shafaq	fegr
day	yevm ; ruz ; gün	yom ; nahar
dead	olü ; mürdey	meyyit
dear (in cost)	pahalu	ghali
deep	derin	'amiq
die	öl–	mat
difficult	müshkil ; güj	mushkil ; sa'b
dig	qaz– ; hafr et–	hafar
dinner	yemek ; ta'am	ghada
dirty	kirli	wesikh
dish	tabaq ; qab	tabaq
district	sanjaq ; qaza	markaz
do	et–	'amal
don't !	mey	la
doctor	hekim ; tabib	hakim
dog	zaghar ; tazi	kelp
donkey	eshek ; khar	hamar
door	qapu ; bab	bab
down	asha	taht
drain	laghim	masraf
dress, a	ruba ; üstbash	libs
drink, to	ich–	shereb
drive, to	git–	saq
drop (let fall)	damla–	waqqa'
duck	ördek	batta
dust	toz	turab

ARABIC (E.)	PERSIAN	HINDUSTANI
mud'lim	mudlim	and'era
tarikh	tarikh	tarikh
bint	dukhtar	beti
fijr	sahar	prab'at
yom ; nahar	ruẓ	din ; roz
meyyit	murd	mar–gaya
ghali	giran	ma'anga
'amiq	darad	gahra
mat ; tawaffa	mir–	mar–ja–
mushkil ; sa'b	moshkil ; sakht	mushkil ; sakht
hafar	kan–	khod–
ghada ; 'asha	sham	khana
wesikh	kasif	maila
ma'un	zarf	rikabi
nahiya	shahrestan	zila
sawwa	kun–	kar–
la	na	mat ——o ; mat karo
hakim ; tabib	hakim ; doktor	doktor
kelp	sag	kutta
hamar ; zamal	khar	gad'a
bab	dar	darwaza
taht ; hadr	pa'in	niche
mejra ; saqia	ab dar–raw	nali
libs	rakht	poshaq ; kapre
shereb	khor– ; nushi–	pi–
saq	ran–	chala–
nezzel	chakani	gira de–
besh	urdak	batak
toz ; 'ajaj	gard	mitti

ENGLISH	TURKISH	ARABIC (W.)
each	her bir	kull
east	sharq	sharq
easy	rahat ; qoley	sehl
eat	ye–	akal
egg	beyza	beda
eight	sekiz	tamanya
eleven	on bir	hidashar
empty	khali	farigh
end	uj ; son	nehaya ; akhir
enemy	düshman ; khasim	’adu
enough	kyafi	bes
enter	gir– ; dakhil ol–	dakhal
envelop	zarf	zarf
evening	akhsham	maghrib
explain	izah et–	fesser
extinguish	utfa et–	taffa
extra	fazla	ziada
eye	göz	’ain
face	yüz ; chehrey	wajh
fall, to	düsh–	weqe’
family	khandaan	’ela
fan	yelpaze	marwaha
far	dur ; uzaq	be’id
farmer	renjber	fallah
fasten	bala–	rabat
fat (stout)	semiz	semin
father	peder	ab ; walid
fear, to	qorq–	khaf
feast	ziyafet ; id	’id

ARABIC (E.)	PERSIAN	HINDUSTANI
kull	har	har ; ek ek
sharq	mashriq	mashriq ; purab
sehl ; heyyin	sahl	asan
akal	khur–	kha–
beda	tukhm	anda
tamanya	hasht	at'
hidashar	yazda	gyara
khali	khali	khali
nehaya	khatima ; sar	khatm; sira; akhir
'adu	doshman ; khasim	dushman
bes ; kafi	bas ; kafi	bas ; khafi
dakhal	dakhil shau–	andar ja–
d'arf	lifafa	lifafa
mesa	sham	sham
fesser	hali kun–	samja–
taffa	khamush kun–	buja–
zayid	foghaladey	faltu
'ain	chashm	ankh
wajh	surat ; ru	chihra
weqe' ; tah	uft–	gir–
'ela	ayal	balbach'e
maheffa	bad bi–zan	pank'a
be'id	dur	dur
fallah	fallahi ; zari	kisan
rabat ; shedd	band–	band–
semin	gunda	mota
ab ; walid	pidar ; valid	bap
khaf	tarsi–	dar–
'id ; diyafa	id ; mihmani	mihmani

ENGLISH	TURKISH	ARABIC (W.)
feed, to	besley–	wakkil
female	dishi ; madey	nitaya
fence	siper	zarbiya
fetch	getir–	gab
fever	hümma	sakhuna
few	az ; qalil	qalil
field	sahra ; tarla	get
fight, to	qavgha et–	taharab
find, to	bul–	leqa
finger	parmaq	sub'
finish	bitir–	khallas
fire	atesh	nar
first	ilk ; birinji	awwel
fish	baliq	semeka
five	besh	khamsa
flag	bairaq	beraq
flat	düz ; yassi	mibattat
flood	sel ; tufan	gharaq
floor	döshemey	ard
flour	un	tehin
flower	chichek	zahra
fly, a	sinek	debana
fog	duman	dabab
fold, to	qatla–	tabbaq
follow	taqib et–	teba'
food	yem ; yeyejek	ta'am ; ekl
foot	pa ; qadem	qadam ; rigl
for (prep.)	ichin	'alashan ; li
foreigner	ejnebi	egnabi
forest	orman	ghaba
forget	unut–	nesi

ARABIC (E.)	PERSIAN	HINDUSTANI
ta'm	khurani–	khila–
nitya	zan ; madey	aurat ; aurat ka–
siyaj	divara	jangla
jab	ar–	la–
sakhuna	tab	bukar ; tap
qalil	kam	kam ; t'ore
mazra'a ; medan	zera'at	khet ; maidan
taharab ; ta'arak	jang kun–	lar–
leqa ; wajad	yab–	pata laga–
sub'a ; usbu'	angusht	ungli
khallas ; kemmel	tamam kun–	khat'm kar–
nar	atash	ag
awwel	avval	pa'la
semeka	mahi	machli
khamsa	panj	panch
beraq	bairaq	j'anda
'adil	musattah	hamwar
zod	sailab	sailab
ard	zamin	farsh
tehin	ard	atta
warad	gul	phul
debana	magas	makhi
dabab	mih	kohra
tawa	ta kun–	tah kar–
teba'	pushti–sar rav–	pich'a kar–
ta'am ; ekl	khurak	khana
qadam ; rijl	pa	paon
li ejel ; khatir	baraye	–ke lie
ejnabi	khareji	ghair–mulkwala
ghaba	jangal	jangal
nesi	faramush kun–	b'ul–

ENGLISH	TURKISH	ARABIC (W.)
fork	chatal	shoka
fort	qala	qal'a
four	dört	arba'a
friend	dost	sahib
from	–den	min
front, in	ön	muqdim
fruit	meyvey	fakha
fry	tavada pishir	qala
fuel	kömür	hatab
garden	baghchey	ginena ; baghcha
gate	qapu	bauwaba
gather	topla–	jema'
gentleman	effendi	efendi ; khawaga
get	al–	gab
girl	qiz	bint
give	ver–	idda
glass (drinking)	bardaq	kubbaya
glass (looking)	ayna	miraya
glove	eldivan	guwanti
goat	kechi	tes
go	git–	rah ; mesh
good	eyi ; ala	tayyib
goods	eshya ; mal	buda'a
god	allah	allah ; ilah
gold	altun	deheb
government	hükümeti	hukuma
gown	fistan ; ruba	fustan
grain	daney	habba
grass	ot	hashish
grave, a	qabr	qabr

ARABIC (E.)	PERSIAN	HINDUSTANI
chingal	changal	kanta
jil'a	qala	qila
arba'a	chahar	char
sadiq	dust	dost
min ; 'an	az	–se
qadam	jilau–i	–ke samne
fakha	mivah	meva ; phal
qala	sorkh kun–	tal–
hatab	hizam	jalne ki chiz
baghcha ; bustan	bagh	bagh ; baghicha
bab	bab	phatak
jema'	jama kun–	jama kar–
efendi ; khawaja	agha	sahib
hassal	yab–	la–
bint	dukhtar	larki
a'ta	dih–	de–
kubbaya ; glass	istikan	glass
aina ; miraya	ayina	aina
keff	dast–kash	dastana
tes ; 'anza	buz	bakri
rah ; mesh	rau–	ja–
tayyib ; zen	khub	ach'a
amwal	asbab ; kala	saman
allah	allah	khuda ; allah
deheb	zar	sona
hukuma	daulat	sarkar ; hukumat
fustan	lebas	jubba
ta'am	dana	dana
hashish	'alaf	ghas
qabr	qabar	qabar

ENGLISH	TURKISH	ARABIC (W.)
grease	yagh	dihn
great	azim ; böyük	kebir
green	yeshil	akhdar
greet	selam ver–	salem 'ala
ground	yer ; arsa	ard
grow	böyü–	nema
guest	müsafir	def
guide	rehber	dalil
gun	tüfeng	bunduqiya
hair	sach ; qil	sha'ra
half	yarim ; nim	nuss
hand	el	yed ; id
handkerchief	mendil	mendil
handle	sap ; qabzey	yed ; id
happen	ol–	jara
happy	sa'adetli	sa'id
hat	shapqa	burneta
he	o	huwa
head	bash ; ser ; res	ras
hear	dinle–ishit–	seme'
heart	qalb ; dil	qalb
heaven	firdevs ; sema	sema
heavy	aghir	teqil
hedge	chit	zarbiya
hen	tavuq	farkha
here	bura	hena
high	yüksek	'ali
hill	depey	tel ; gebel
hire, to	kirala–	kera
his	onun	–u

ARABIC (E.)	PERSIAN	HINDUSTANI
dihn	gris ; dihn	charbi
kebir ; ad'im	buzurg	bara
akhdar	sabz	hara
salem 'ala	salam dih–	salam de–
ard	zam ; zamin	zamin
nema	ruy–	ug–
def	mihman	mihman
dalil ; museyyir	rahbar	ra'numa
tufka	tofang	banduq
sha'ra	mu	bal
nus'f	nim	ad'a
yed ; id	dast	hat'
mendil ; kefiya	dastmal	rumal
yed ; id	dastgirey	karri ; handal
jara ; sar	shau– ; bash–	ho–
sa'id ; masrur	khush–vaqt	khush
shefqa ; qapus	kulah	topi
huwa	in	wuh
ras	sar	sir
seme'	shinav–	sun–
qalb	dil	dil
sema	firdaus	firdaus ; bihisht
teqil	sangin	b'ari
siyaj	kharband	j'arbandi
dujaja	makiyan	murghi
hena	inja	y'han ; id'r
'ali	buland ; ali	uncha
tel ; jebel	tappah	pahari
kera	kiraya gir–	kiraye par le–
–u	–esh	uska

ENGLISH	TURKISH	ARABIC (W.)
home	ev ; vatan	bet
home, at	evdey	istaqbil
honest	emin ; sadiq	amin ; sadiq
honey	bal ; mikh ; asal	'asal
hope, to	ümmid et–	it'assim
horse	esb ; at	husan
hospital	khastakhane	isbitalya
hot	sijaq	harr
hotel	khan	loqanda
hour	sa'at	sa'a
house	ev ; beyt	beyt
how ?	nijey	kef
how much ?	ne'qadar	kam
hundred, a	yüz	mia
hunt, to	avla–	ed
hurt, to	injit–	aza
husband	qoja	goz
hut	qulübe	'issa
I	ben	ana
if	eyer	law
ill	meriz ; hasta	marid'
immediately	o sa'at	halan
important	muhim	muhim
ink	mürekkeb	hebr
inn	khan	khan
insect	böjek	hashara
interpreter	müterjim	turguman
into	–e	fi
iron	demir	hadid

ARABIC (E.)	PERSIAN	HINDUSTANI
bet	khana	ghar
fil bet	khana	ghar men
amin ; sadiq	amin	imandar
'asal	asal ; mikh	shahd
te–emmel	ummid dar–	umed kar–
husan	asb	g'ora
khastakhana	marizkhana	aspital
harr	garm	garm
loqanda	mihman–khana	hotel ; sarai
sa'a	sa'at	g'anta
beyt	khana ; manzel	makan
kef	che taur	kis tarah
sh'qadr	chi–qadr ; chand	kitna
mia	sau	sau ; ek sau
ed	shikar kun–	shikar kar–
'awwar	zakhm kun–	nuqsan kar–
zoj ; rejul	shauhar	khawind
sarifa	kulba	basti
ana	bande	main
law ; id'a	agar	agar
marid' ; khasta	mariz ; nakhosh	bimar
halan ; bis sa'a	fauran	ek dam ; fauran
muhim	lazim	zaruri
hebr	murakkab	siahi
khan	sarai ; mihmankhana	sarai
baqq	hashrat	kira
turjuman	tarjuman	tarjuman
fi	tu ; dar	–men
hadid	ahin	loha

ENGLISH	TURKISH	ARABIC (W.)
is	dir	—
is not	deyil'dir	—
island	jezire	gezira
it	o	huwa
jewel	jevahir	gohara
journey	seyahat	sefer
judge, a	qadi ; hakim	qad'i
jug	desti	briq
jump, to	sichra–	natt
juice	su	'asir
kettle	gügüm	abriq
key	miftah	miftah
kick, to	tep–	refes
kill	öldür–	qatal
kind (amiable)	tatli	safuq
kind (sort)	jins	gins
king	q'ral ; padishah	melek
kitchen	ashkhane ; matbakh	matbakh
knife	bichaq	sikkina
know, to	bil–	dere ; 'eref
lady	hanim	hanim ; sitt
lake	göl	buhera
lamb	quzu	kharuf
lamp	lamba	lamba ; qandil
land	qara	ard ; mulk
lane	yol	'atfa

ARABIC (E.)	PERSIAN	HINDUSTANI
—	ast	hai ; he
—	nist	ne'hai
jezira	jazira	jazira
huwa	an ; in	wuh
johara	javahir	jawahir
sefer	safar	safar
qad'i	ghazi	insaf
briq ; jak	kuze	kuza
tafar	jastan kun–	kud–
'asir	shira ; ab	ras
kidr	ketri	kitli
miftah	kalid	chabi
refes	lagad zan–	lat mar–
qatal	kush–	mar dal–
latif	az rahi lutf	mihrban
jins	jur ; gune	qism
melek	shah ; padshah	raja ; badishah
matbakh	ashpaz–khana	bawarchi–khana
sikkina	kard	ch'uri
dere ; 'eref	dan– ; shinas–	jan– ; –ko malum ho–
khatun	khanom	begam ; memsah'b
buhera	daryacha	j'il ; talab
tali	barra	b'er ka bach'a
lampa	chiragh	batti
ard ; mulk	zam ; zamin	zamin
shari'	kucha	gali ; kucha

ENGLISH	TURKISH	ARABIC (W).
language	zeban ; lisan	lisan
large	iri ; böyük	kebir
last	son	akhir
late	gej ; sabiq	mitakher
laugh, to	gül–	dehek
law	qanun ; shariyat	qanun
lawyer	vekili ; avoqat	abukato
lead, to	götür–	dall
leaf	yapraq	warqa
learn	tahsil et–	ta'allam
leave (of absence)	tatil	rukhsa
left (side)	sol	shemal
leg	bajaq	rigl
lend	ödünj ver–	sallif
less	az	aqall
letter	mektub	maktub ; khatt
lie down	yat–	raqad
lift, to	qaldir–	rafa'
light, a	nur	nur
light, to	yaq–	walla'
light (weight)	hafif	khafif
line	chizgi ; khatt	khatt
listen	dinley–	istanat
little, a	bir az	shwaya
live	yasha–	'ash
lock	kilid	qifl
long (distance)	uzun	tawil
lose	yitir–	dayya
love	muhabbet	habb

ARABIC (E.)	PERSIAN	HINDUSTANI
lisan	zeban	zaban
kebir	buzurg	bara se
akhir	akhir	pichla ; akhiri
mitakher	mu'attal ; dir	der se
dahak	khand–	hans–
qanun ; shar'	qanun	qanun ; qaida
wakil da'wa	qanun–dan	vakil
qad	bar–	rah bata–
warqa	barg	patta
ta'allam	yad gir–	sikh–
rukhsa	murakh–khasi	ch'utti
shemal	chap	baen
rijl	saq	tang
aqrad'	qarz dih–	qarz de–
aqall	kam	kam
maktub ; khatt	kaghaz	chitt'i
nam	khwabi–	let–
rafa'; shal	buland kun–	ut'a–
nur	chiragh	roshni
sha'al	rushan kun–	jala–
khafif	khafif	halka
khatt ; satr	khatt	lakir
istema'	gush dih–	sun–
shweya ; qalil	kami	t'ora
seken ; 'ash	zi–	ji–; rah–
qifl	qufl	tala
tawil	daraz ; boland	lamba
deyya	gum kun–	gum kar–
habb	dust dar–	piyar kar–

ENGLISH	TURKISH	ARABIC (W.)
low	alchaq	wati
madam	hanim; madama	sitt ; madama
make	yap–; imal et–	’amal
man	insan ; adam	insan ; ragil
many	choq	ketir
map	kharta	kharta
market	pazar	suq
marriage	nikyah	gawaz
master	effendi ; agha	sid
mat	hasir	hasira
match	kibrit	kibrit
mattress	minder	farsha
me	beni	–ni ; –i
meat	et	lahm
medicine	deva	dawa
meet	rastgel–	laqa
meeting	ijtima	igtima’
mend	tamir–	sallah
merchant	tajir	tajir
midnight	geje yarusu	nuss el lel
milk	süd	halib
minute	daqiqa	daqiqa
mistake	khata	ghilit
money	aqjey	fulus
monkey	maimun	qird
month	shahr ; mah	shahr
moon	qamer ; mah	qamr
more	ziadey	ezyed ; aktar
morning	sabah	subh ; sabah

ARABIC (E.)	PERSIAN	HINDUSTANI
nasi	pa'in	nicha
sitt	khanom	begam ; memsahib
sawwa	saz–	bana–; kar–
rejil ; adami	mard	admi
ketir ; wajid	khaili	ba'ut
kharita	naqsha	naqsha
suq	bazar	bazar
'urs	'arusi	shadi
ra'is	arbab	malik ; sah'b
hasira	burya	chatai
kibrit	kibrit	kari ; machis
doshek	dushak	gadela
–ni ; –i	–am	mujh(e)
lahm	gusht	gosht
dawa	dava	dawa
laqa ; ijtema	mulaqat kun–	–se mil–
ijtima'	majlis	jalus
sallah	durust kun–	maramat kar-
tajir	tajir	saudagar
nuss el lel	nim–shab	ad'i rat
halib	shir	dud'
daqiqa	daqiqa	minit
ghelet	estebah	galti
fulus	pul	paisa
shadi	buzinah	bandar
shahr	mah	ma'ina
qamr	mah	chand
ezyed ; aktar	bishtar	ziada ; aur
subh ; sabah	subh	subah

ENGLISH	TURKISH	ARABIC (W.)
mosque	jami ; mesjid	gami ; masgid
most	en ziadey	el ekter
mother	mader ; ana	umm
motor-car	otomobil	tambil
mountain	jebel	gebel
mouth	aghiz ; dihan	fumm
move, to	qimildan–	harrak
Mr.	–effendi	khawaga
Mrs.	–hanim	sitt
much	choq	ketir
mud	chamur	tin
mule	qatir	baghl
music	musiqa	muziqa
my	benim	–i
nail (iron)	ekser ; mikh	musmar
name	ad ; isim ; nam	ism
narrow	dar	dayyiq
nation	millet ; ummet	umma
near	yaqin	qarib
nearly	heman	taqriban
necessary	lazim	lazm ; daruri
needle	iyney	ibra
never	hich ; asla	ebeden
new	yeni ; jedid	gedid
news	khaber	khabr
newspaper	gazeta	garida
next	yandaki	tani
night	gejey	lel

ARABIC (E.)	PERSIAN	HINDUSTANI
jami ; masjid	masjid	masjid
el ekter ; ezyed	–tar az hama	sab se–
umm ; walida	madar	man
tambil	otomobil	motor–gari ; gari
jebel	kuh	pahar
halq ; fah	dahan	munh
harrak	harakat kun–	chal–
khawaga	agha–yi–	–sah'b
sitt	khanom–i–	–sah'ba
ketir	khaili	ba'ut
tin ; wahl	gel	mitti
baghl	qatir	khach'ar
muziqa	musiqan	baja
–i	–am	mer'
bismar	mikh	mekh
ism	ism ; nam	nam
dayyiq	tang	tang
umma	daulat ; kashvar	qaum ; jat
qarib	qarib ; nazdik	nazdik
taqriban	taqriban	taqriban ; qarib–qarib
lazm ; daruri	lazem	zaruri
ibra	suzan	sui
abadan	hich ; hargiz na	kab'i na'in
jedid	nau	naya
khabr	khabar	khabar
jarida	ruznama ; akhbar	akhbar
tani ; thumma	ayanda	agla
lel	shab	rat

ENGLISH	TURKISH	ARABIC (W.)
nine	doquz	tis'a
no	khair ; hich	ma ; la
noon	öylen	duhr
north	shimal	shimal
nose	burun	manakhir
not	deyil	la ; ma ; mush
nothing	hich	la she ; mafish haga
now	shimdi ; elan	dilwaqt ; alan
number	sayi ; aded	'add
o'clock	sa'at	es sa'a
of	–in	–; min
office	idarekhane	diwan
officer	zabiti ; mamur	dabit ; mamur
often	ekseriya	marrat kitira
oil	yagh	zet
O.K. (all right)	eyi ; vesselam	tayyib ; zen
old	esgi	qadim ; 'aguz
on	–de	'ala
once	bir kerrey	marra
one	bir	wahid
only	salt ; anjaq	bes ; faqat
open	achiq	maftuh
or	ya	aw
orange	portuqal ; narenj	burtugana ; naringa
order, to	emr et–	amar
other	akher ; diger	akhar
our	bizim	–na
out	dishari	barra

ARABIC (E.)	PERSIAN	HINDUSTANI
tis'a	nuh	nau
lakhair ; ma ; la	khair	na'in ; ney
duhr	zuhr	do pahar
shimal	shamal	shimal
khashm	demagh	nak
la ; ma ; mush	khair ; na	na'in ; ney
hich ; la she	hich na	kuch na'in
alan ; hessa	hala	ab'i
'add	numra	tadad ; nam'r
es sa'a	sa'at–i	baje
—	–i	–ka ; –ki
idara	idareh	daft'r ; ofis
dabit ; mamur	afsar	afsar ; sardar
wajid ; kathir	aksar	aksar; ba'ut dafa
gaz ; dihn	raughan	tel
tayyib ; zen	khaili khub	t'ik 'e ; ach'a
kabir ; 'atiq	kuhna	purana ; bud'a
'ala	bar ; ru	–par
marra	yak dafa	ek dafa
wahid	yak	ek
bes ; faqat	faqat	sirf ; k'ali
maftuh	baz	khola
aw ; yo	ya	ya
portugala	narangi	narangi
amar	hukm kun–	hukm de–
akhar	digar	dusra
–na	–a man	hamar'
barra	birun	bahar

ENGLISH	TURKISH	ARABIC (W).
pack up	sar–	hazam
pain	aghri ; sizi	waga'
paper	kisd	waraq
path	yol ; tariq	sikka
pay, to	öde–	dafa'
peace	musaleha	sulh ; salam
pen	qalem	qalem
pencil	qurshun qalem	qal'm rasas
people	millet ; qavm	nas
pepper	biber	filfil
perfume	rayiha	'etr
person	shakhs ; adem	shakhs
picture	tasvir ; resim	sura
pig	donuz	khanzir
pillow	yastiq	makhadda
pin	toplu	dabbus
pineapple	ananas	ananas
pipe	chibuq	shubuk
place	yer	makan ; mahall
plain (ground)	ova	sahl
plant, a	fidan	nabat
plate	tabaq ; qab	sahn
play, to	oyna–	le'eb
pocket	jeb	geb
poisonous	zehir	musim
policeman	polis	'askari bolis
pond	göl ; havuz	birka
pony	midilli	sisi
porter	hammal	hammal
possess	malik ol–	melek

ARABIC (E.)	PERSIAN	HINDUSTANI
lemm	band–	band kar–
waja'	dard	dard
kaghid	kaghaz	kagaz
sikka	rah	pagdandi
wafa	pul dih–	talab de–; paisa de–
sulh ; salam	sulah ; salam	sulah ; aram
qalem	qalam	qalam
qal'm rasas	madad	pensil
nas ; shali	mardum	log
filfil	filfil	mirch
'etr	etr	khushbu
shakhs	shakhs	shakhs
sura ; resm	taswir	taswir
khanzir	khenzir	suar
makhadda	balish	takiya
debbus	sanjaq	tachni
ananas	ananas	ananas
sabil	chupuq	huqa ; nali
makan ; mahall	makan ; ja	jagah
chol ; barriya	medan ; dasht	maidan
nabat	rustani	pauda
sahn	bushqab	rikabi
la'ab	bazi–	khel–
jeb	jib	jeb
musim	zahrdar	zahrila
'askari bolis	azhan ; pazban	poliswala
birka	hauz	johar ; talab
sisi	yabu	tattu
hammal	hammal	kuli ; hammal
malek	dar	(see note)

ENGLISH	TURKISH	ARABIC (W.)
post office	postahane	maktab bosta
pot	chanaq ; qab	qidr
potato	patates	batatsa
pour	dök–	kabb
prayer	niyaz ; rija	sạlwa
present, to be	bulun–	hidir
price	qimet ; fiyat	taman ; qima
priest	keshish ; papas	qassis
prince	bey ; shahzadey	emir ; saltan
prisoner	esir ; mahbes	mahbus
profession	san'at	iqrar
pull	chek–	garr
punish	mujazat et–	qasas
purse	kesey	kis
put	qo–; vaz et–	hatt
quarter	rub	rub'
question	sival	suwal
quick	tez ; chapuq	sari'
rabbit	tavshan	arnab
rain	yaghmur	matr
raisins	chamish	zabib
rat	gerel	far
railway	demir–yol	sikka hadid
raw	chi	ni
razor	ustura	mus
read, to	oqu–	qara
ready	hazir	hadir
receipt	maqbuz	wasl
red	qirmizi	ahmar

ARABIC (E.)	PERSIAN	HINDUSTANI
bostakhana	post–khana	dak–khana
jidr ; hibb	dik	bartan ; lota
bateta	sib–i–zamini	alu
sabb	riz–	dal–
sala	namaz	namaz ; puja
had'ar	tashrif dar–	hazir ho–
qima ; si'r	qimat	qimat
qass	pir ; murshid	mulla ; pujari
amir ; saltan	amir ; shahzada	raja ; maharaja
mahbus ; asir	dastgir ; pisha	qaidi
wadifa	estekhdam	pesha
jarr	kash–	khench–
qasas	saza dih–	saza de–
kis	kisah	t'aili ; kis
hatt	nih–; guzar–	rakh–
rub'	rub	pao
suwal	so'al	sawal
sari'; khafif	zud	jaldi ; tez
arnab	khargush	khargosh
matr	barish	barish
zabib	kishmish	kishmish
juredi	mush	chuha
sikka hadid ; rel	relwey	rel
ni	kham	kach'a
mus	tigh	ustura
qara	khan–	par'–
hadir	hazir	taiyar
wasl	rasid	rasid
ahmar	sorkh	lal

ENGLISH	TURKISH	ARABIC (W.)
relation	aqriba	qarib
remember	der khatir et–	itzakkar
remove	qaldir–	shal
repair, to	tamir et–	sallah
reply, to	jevab ver–	gawab
rescue, to	qurtar–	khallas
rest (repose)	rahat	raha
return (go back)	dön–	rigi
rice (raw)	pirinj	ruzz ; shileb
rice (cooked)	pilav	ruzz ; timen
rich	zengin	ghani
ride, to	bin–	rekeb
rifle	tüfeng	bunduqiya
right (side)	sagh taraf	yamin
right (correct)	haq ; doghru	sahih
ripe	olmush	mustawi
rise, to	qalq–; yuksel–	qam
river	irmaq ; nehr	nahr
road	yol ; ṣaddey	sikka ; tariq
roof	dam	sat'
room	oda	oda
rope	ip ; halat	habl
rotten	chürük	mi'affin
rough	qaba	khashm
rug	kechey ; kilim	sagada ; zuliya
run	qosh–	giri
sack	chuval	kis
safe	emin ; salim	emin ; salim
salt	tuz	melh
same	zat	zat
sand	qum	raml

ARABIC (E.)	PERSIAN	HINDUSTANI
qarib	khish	rishtadar
tedekker	yad dar–	yad kar–
shal	bar–	leja–
'ammar	durust kun–	maramat kar–
jawab	jawab kun–	jawab de–
khallas	khalas kun–	bacha–
raha	aram	aram
rejey	bar-gard–	wapas ja–
shileb	birinj	chawal
timen	birinj ; pilau	b'at
ghani ; zengin	ghani	amir
rekeb	savar kun–	sowar kar–
tufka ; matli	tofang	raif'l ; banduq
yamin	rast	da'ina
munasib; tamam	durust	t'ik ; durust
mustawi	rasida	pakka
qam ; sa'ad	pa–shau–	ut'–
nahr ; shatt	rud–khana	darya
tariq ; darb	rah	rasta
sat'	bam	ch'atri
gubba ; ghurfa	utaq	kamra
habl	tanab	rassi
fasid	pusida	sara hua ; k'rab
khashm	zebr	khurdura ; kach'a
sajada ; zuliya	qalicha	dari ; qalicha
reked'	dav–	daur–
goniya	guni	bori ; guni
amin ; salim	iman	salamat
melh	namak	nimak
zat	hamin	ek jaisa
raml	rig	ret

ENGLISH	TURKISH	ARABIC (W.)
sandals	sandal	na'al
sauce	salcha	marqa
savage	yəbani ; vahshi	mitwahish
say	de–	qal
scissors	maqas	maqas
school	mekteb	medresa ; mekteb
screen	perdey	sitara
screw	vida	barrima
sea	deniz	bahr
seat	yer	matrah
second	ikinji	tani
see	gör–	shaf
seek	ara–	dawwar ala
sell	sat–	ba'
send	gönder–	ba'at
seven	yedi	seb'a
several	bir qach	ketir
sew	dik–	khayyat
shallow	sigh	mush gawit
shave, to	trash et–	meyyen
shawl	shal	shal
sheep	qoyun	ghanama
she	o	hiya
sheet	charshaf	farkh
ship	gemi	markab
shirt	gömlek	qamis
shoe	qundura	markub
shoot, to	at-; vur–	darab
shop	dukkian ; maghaza	dukan

ARABIC (E.)	PERSIAN	HINDUSTANI
na'al	give	champal ; chapli
marqa ; sas	chashni	chatni
wahshi	vahshi	jangli
qal	gu–	bol–; kah–
maqas	qaichi	qainchi
maktab; medresa	madrasa	madrassa; skul
hajiz	parda	parda ; chiq
burghi	pich	pech ; skru
bahr	bahr ; darya	samundar
kursi ; skamli	ja	chauki ; kursi
tani	duvum	dusra
shaf	bin–	dek–
dawwar ala	ju–	talash kar–
ba'	farush–	bech–
ba'at	firist–	b'ej–
seb'a	haft	sat'
ketir ; 'adid	chand	ba'ut ; chand
khayyat	duz–	si–
gesh ; ma qalil	kam amiq	ch'ichla ; t'ora
meyyen	tarashi–	hajamat bana–
shal	shal	shal
ghanama; kebsh	gusfand	b'er
hiya	in ; an	wuh
charchafm warqa	chadar	chadar
markab; safina	jahaz	jahaz
qamis	pirahan	kamis
qandara	kafsh	juti
rama	tir andaz	goli mar–
dukan	dukan	dukan

ENGLISH	TURKISH	ARABIC (W.)
short	qisa	qasir
shoulder	umuz	qitf
shout, to	bar–	sah
show, to	baqit–	beyyen ; shawaf
side	janib ; taraf	ganib
sign	alamet ; nishan	'alama
sign, to	imzala–	emda
silk	ipek	harir
silver	gümüsh	fedda
since	beri	min waqt
sir	effendi	effendim
sister	hemshirey	ukht
sit	otur–	qa'ad
six	alti	sitta
skin	deri	giled
skirt	etek	tanura
sky	gök yüzü	sema
sleep, to	uyu–	nam
slow	aghir ; bati	mitani ; bati
small	küchük; saghir	sughair
smell, a	qoqu	riha ; shemm
smoke	düman	dukhan
smoke, to	tüt–	sharab dukhan
snake	yilan	ti'ban
snow	qar	tel'g
so	öyle	keda
soap	sabun	sabun
socks	chorab	shurab
soft	yumshaq	na'im
soil	pislik	ard ; turab

ARABIC (E.)	PERSIAN	HINDUSTANI
qasir	kutah	ch'ota ; kami
qitf	shanah	kand'a
sah	seyah kun–	chilla–
beyyen ; rawa	nama–	dikha–
janib	pahlu	kinara ; taraf
'alama	nishan	nishan
emda	emza kun–	dastkhat kar–
harir ; ibrisam	abrishami	resham
fedda	nuqra	chandi
min ; madam	chun	–se
effendim	agha	sah'b
ukht	hemshire ; khahar	bahin
qa'ad	nishin-	bait'–
sitta	shish	ch'e
jiled	pust	khal
tanura	daman	daman
sema	aseman	asman
nam	khab–	so–
thaqil ; bati	ahista	a'ista
sughair	kuchik	ch'ota
riha ; shemm	bu	bu
dukhan	dokhan	d'uan
sharab titen	kashi–	(tambaqu) pi–
hayya	mar	sanp
tel'j	barf	barf
hakeda	antor	aisa
sabun	sabun	sabun
jawarib	jurab	moze
leyyin	narm	narm
ard ; turab	khak	mitti

ENGLISH	TURKISH	ARABIC (W.)
soldier	asker ; nefer	'askari
some	bir qach	ba'd
something	bir she	she
sometimes	ba'zi defa	fi ba'd el ahyan
son	oghul	ibn
song	türkü ; mani	ginwa
soon	bir azdan	halan
sorry	mükedder	haznan
sort	soi ; dürlü	gins
soup	chorba	shorba
sour	ekshi	hamid
south	jenub ; qibley	ginub
speak	qonush–	haka ; tekelem
spectacles	güzlik	manzar
spend	sarf et–; kharja–	saraf
spices	baharat	baharat
spoon	qashiq	ma'laqa
spring, a	punar ; bahar	'ain
stable	tavla	tola ; istabl
stairs	merdiven	salalim
stamp (postal)	pul	bul ; tabi' bosta
stand, to	dur–	qam
star	yildiz ; sitare	negma
starch	qola	nisha
start, to	yola chiq–	mesha ; ibteda
station, police	meuqi	karakol
station, railway	istasyon	mahatta
stay, to	qal– ; otur–	baqa
steal	chal–	saraq ; bakhira

ARABIC (E.)	PERSIAN	HINDUSTANI
'askari	sarbaz	sipa'i
ba'd ; she	qadri ; chand	kuch'
she ; ferd she	chiz–i	kuch na kuch'
ba'd waqt	gah gah–i	kabi kabi
ibn	pisar ; walad	beta
naghma ; pesta	avaza	git ; gana
bil 'ajel ; halan	zud	jald ; jaldi se
mute–essif	mota–asef	afsos se
jins	jur ; gune	qism
shorba	shurva ; ab–i–gusht	shorva
hamid	talkh	khatta
jinub	junub	janub
haka ; tekelem	gu–	bol–; kah–
mand'ara	enak	chashma
saraf	kharj kun–	kharch kar–
baharat	adviya	masala
khashuga	qashuq	chamcha
'ain	chasma	chashma
tola	tavila	astbal
derej	pilla	sirhi
bul	tamr	tikat
qam	ist–	khara ho–
nejma	setara	tara ; istara
nisha	nishasta	kalaf
mesha ; ibteda	shuru kun–	shuru kar–
markaz polis	kalantari	t'ana
mahatta	istgah	isteshan
baqa	man–	rah–
saraq ; baq	duzd–	chura–

ENGLISH	TURKISH	ARABIC (W.)
steamer	vapor	markab bukhar
steel	chelik	bulad
stick	deynek	'ud
sting, a	iney	las'a
stocking	chorab	shurab
stomach	mi'de	mi'da
stone	tash	hagar
stop, to	dur	waqaf
storm	furtuna	zoba'a
story	hikiaya	hikaya
straight	doghru	elil gubal
stranger	gharib	gharib
street	soqaq ; mahalle	sikka ; shari'
strike, to	vur–	darab
string	ip ; sijim	khait
strong	quvvetli	qawi
study, to	chalush–	deres
sugar	sheker	sukkar
summer	yaz	sef
sun	günesh	shems
supper	akhsham ta'ami	'asha
swamp	batqluq	mustanqa
swim	yüz–	am
table	sofra ; masa	sufra ; mez
tailor	terzi	khayyat
take away	al– ; qaldir–	shall
take (hold of)	al– ; zabt et–	misik
talk, to	laqirdi et–	haka
tank (reservoir)	sahrunj	hud ; tanka

ARABIC (E.)	PERSIAN	HINDUSTANI
markab dukhan	kashti–yi–bukhar	jahaz
fulad	pulad	faulad
'asa	chub	lakri
las'a	nish	dank
jawarib	jurab	jurab
meda	shikam	pet
hajar	sang	pat'ar
waqaf	va ist–	rok–
fortona	tufan	tufan
hikaya	qissa	qissa
elil jubal	rast	sid'a
gharib	ajnabi	ajnabi
shari' ; darb	kheyaban	rasta ; gali
darab	zan–	mar–
khait ; sutli	risman	d'aga
qawi	ghavi	mazbut
deres ; tala'	amuz	ghaur kar ; sikh–
sheker	shakkar	chini ; shakkar
sef	tabistan	garmi (mausim)
shems	aftab	suraj
'asha	sham	rat ka khana
hor	mashila	daldal ; j'il
sebeh	shena kun–	tair–
mez	miz	mez
khayyat	khayyat	derzi
wada	bar–	leja–
lezem ; qad'	gir–	qabu kar– ; le–
haka	gu– ; guftugu kun–	bol–
hud ; tanka	hauz ; daryacha	talab

ENGLISH	TURKISH	ARABIC (W.)
tea	chai	chai
teach	talim et–	allam
teacher	muallim ; hoja	muallim
telegram	telegraf	telghraf
tell, to	söile– ; de–	qal ; khabbar
temple	heykel ; ma'bed	hekal
ten	on	ash'ra
tent	chadir	khema
than	–dan	min
that	o ; shu	ili ; dikha
their	–lari ; anlerin	–hum
then	sonra ; badehu	waqtaha
there	ora	hinak
therefore	imdi	lid'alik
they	onlar	huma ; hum
thick	qalin ; siq	takhin
thief	khirsiz	harami ; sariq
thin	injo	rafi'
thing	ish ; shey	she ; haga
think	düshün	ifteker
this	bu ; shu	da
thousand	bin	elf
thread	tel ; iplik	khait
three	üch	talata
throw, to	at	rama
ticket	bilet	teskera
tie, to	baghla–	rabat–
time	vaqit	waqt
tin	qalai ; tenekc	teneka

ARABIC (E.)	PERSIAN	HINDUSTANI
chai	chai	chai ; cha
allam	dars dih–	sikha–
muallim	muallam	ustad ; guru ; munshi
teleghraf	talagraf	tar
haka	gu–	bata–
hekal	ma'bad	mandir ; gurdwara
ash'ra	dah	das
khema	khaima ; chador	tambu
min	az	–se
ili ; had'ak el	an	wuh
–hum	–ishan	unka
t'umma	pas	to
hinak	anja	wahan
lid'alik	ta	islie
huma ; hum	anha	wuh
takhin ; matin	kuluft	mota ; ghana
sariq ; bawaq	dozd	chor
raqiq ; khafif	nazuk	patla
she ; amr	amr ; chiz	chiz ; bat
ifteker	khiyal kun–	khayal kar–
hada	in	yih
elf	hazar	hazar
khait	risman	sut
talata	si	tin
rama ; deb	andaz–	phenk–
teskera	tikit	tikit
rabat ; shed	band–	band–
waqt	vaqt	waqt
teneka	ghuti	tin ; daba

ENGLISH	TURKISH	ARABIC (W.)
to	–e ; –a	ila ; li
today	bu gün	en naharda
together	beraber	wiya ba'd
tomorrow	yarin	bukra
tonight	bu akhsham	el lela
too (much)	ziyade	bizyada
tooth	dish	sinn
torch	meshala	mash'al
touch, to	doqun–	lamas
towards	doghru	li gihet
towel	havli	beshkir
tower	kuley ; burj	burg
town	shehir	belad
track	yol	sikka
trade, to	tijaret et–	tagar
train (railway)	demir yol qatari	qatr
translate, to	terjeme et–	targam
travel, to	seyahat et–	safar
traveller	seyah	musafir ; sayih
tree	aghaj	shegera
tribe	qabile	qabila
trousers	don ; shalvar	bantalon
true	doghru	sahih ; haqiqi
try, to	chalish–	garrab
turban	sariq	imma
twelve	on iki	itnashar
twenty	yirmi	'ashrin
twice	iki def'a	marraten
two	iki	itnen
umbrella	shemsiye	shemsiya

ARABIC (E.)	PERSIAN	HINDUSTANI
ila ; li	bi	–ko
helyom	amruz	aj
wiya ba'd	hamra	ek sat'
bukra	farda	kal
el lela	amshab	aj ratko
zayid	khaili	ba'ut ; ziada
sinn	dandan	dant
mash'al	mash'al	batti
jas	zan–	ch'u– ; hat laga–
ila tar'f	bi taraf–i	–ki taraf
beshkir	dastmal	tauliya
burj	burj	burj ; minar
belad	shahr	shahr
sikka	rah	pagdandi
tajar ; bedel	tijarat kun–	beopar kar–
qaṭr ; tren	ghetar	rail–gari
tarjam	tarjuma kun–	tarjuma kar–
safar	safar kun–	safar kar–
musafir	musafir	musafir
shejera	darakht	darakht
'ashira ; qabila	il	qaum ; jat
pantalon ; sirwal	shalvar	patlun ; paijama
sahih ; haqiqi	sahih ; rast	sach
jarrab	kushish kun–	koshish kar–
im'ma ; lefa	pagri	pagri
itnashar	duwazda	bara'
'ashrin	bist	bis
marraten	do dafa	do dafa
itnen	do	do
shemsiya	chatr	ch'atri

ENGLISH	TURKISH	ARABIC (W.)
under	alt ; dib	taht
understand	fehm et–	fehem
uniform	uniforma	kiswet et tasrifa
up	bala	foq
us	bizi	–na
useful	faideli	mufid
valley	dere	wadi
value	qimet	qima
vegetables	sebzevat	khadarat
veil	yashmaq	burqu
very	pek	ketir
village	köi	balad
visit, to	ziyaret et–	zar
wages	üjret ; ailiq	shariya
wait, to	bekle–	istanna
wake, to	uyandir–	sahha
walk, to	yörü	meshi
wall	divar ; hisar	hait ; tof
want, to	iste–	'az
war	qavga ; harb	harb
warm	sijaq	dafi
was	idi	kan ; kunet
wash, to	yiqa–	ghasal
washerman	chamashurju	ghasala
watch (clock)	sa'at	sa'a
watch, to	gözle–	gafar
watchman	bekji	gafir

ARABIC (E.)	PERSIAN	HINDUSTANI
taht ; hadr	zir–i	–ke niche
fehem	fahm ; multafit shau–	samaj–
hudum resmiya	uniforma	wardi
foq	bala	upar
–na	–aman	hamko
mufid ; nefa	mufid	kam ka
wadi	tang	wadi ; dara
qima ; temen	qimat	qimat ; dam
khadarat	sabzi	sabzi
pushi	chador	burqa
ketir ; kullish	khaili	ba'ut
qarya ; koi	dih	gaon
zar	zeyarat kun–	mulaqat kar–
shariya ; yomiya	mavajib	talab
istandar	sabr kun–	t'air–
wa'a	bidar kun–	jaga– ; jag'ut–
meshi	piyada rau–	paidal ja–
hait ; tof	diwar	diwar
rad ; 'az	khah–	chah– ; mang
harb	jang	jang ; larai
dafi ; fatir	garm	garm
kan ; kunet	bud	t'a
ghasal	shur–	d'o–
ghasala	rakht–shur ; gazir	d'obi
sa'a	sa'at	g'ari
natar	negar kun–	nazar rakh–
natur	tofangchi	chaukidar

ENGLISH	TURKISH	ARABIC (W.)
water	su	maya
water, drinking	ichilir su	maya hilwa
way	yol	sikka ; tariq
we	biz	ehna
weak	zayif ; hafif	da'if
weapon	silah	silah
week	hafta	goma'
were	idiler	kanu
west	gharb	gharb
wet	islaq ; yash	mablul
what ?	ney	ey ; esh
wheel	tekerlek ; charkh	charkh ; 'agala
when ?	ne vaqit	lamma
where ?	ney rey	fen
which ?	han'gi	min
white	aq ; beyaz	abyad
who ?	kim	min
why ?	ney ichin	ley
wide	enli ; genish	'arid
wife	qari	mara ; ginab el khatun
will (shall)	–jek–	—
wind (air)	yel ; ruzgiar	hawa
window	penjerey	shibbak
wine	sharab	sharab ; nibit
winter	qish	shita
wire	tel	silk ; tel
with	–ley	ma ; bi ; wiya
without	–siz	bi dun
woman	qari	mara

ARABIC (E.)	PERSIAN	HINDUSTANI
maya	ab	pani
maya hilwa	ab baraye	pine ka pani
tariq ; darb	rah	rasta
ehna	ma	ham (log)
da'if	da'if	kamzor
silah	aslehe	hat'yar
joma' ; usbu'	hafta	hafta
kanu	budand	t'e
gharb	maghrib	maghrib ; pach'im
murtib ; nedi	tar	b'iga
esh ; shinu	chi	kya
charkh	charkh	pahiya ; chakkar
yinta ; metta	ke	kab
wen ; en	kuja	k'han ; kid'r
yahu ; ya ; e	kudam	kaunsa
abyad	safid	safed
min	ki	kaun
lesh	chira	kiswaste
'arid	pahn	chaura
harma ; zoja ; jinab el khatun	zan	biwi ; sat'i
—	khahad	-ega
hawa	hawa ; bad	hawa
shubbak	daricha	k'irki
sharab	sharab	sharab
shita	zamistan	sardi
tel ; sim	sim	tar
ma ; bi ; wiya	ba	-se ; -ke sath
bi dun ; bila	bi- ; baghair az	-ke bagair
mara ; harma	zan	aurat

ENGLISH	TURKISH	ARABIC (W.)
wood	aghaj ; odun	khashab
word	söz ; kelam ; lafz	kelema
work (noun)	amel ; ish	shughl
workman	ameley ; ishji	sanayi
worse	dah'a kötü ; beter	arda
worship	ibadet	abada ; sala
wound, a	yara	garh
wrap up	sar–	lef
write	yaz– ; tahrir et–	keteb
wrong	yanlish ; khata	maghlut
year	yil ; seney ; sal	sana
yellow	sari	asfar
yes	evet ; beli	aiwa ; na'am
yesterday	dün	embareh
you	siz	enta
young	genj ; dahil	sughair
your	–iniz ; sizin	–ek ; –kum

ARABIC (E)	PERSIAN	HINDUSTANI
khashab	chub	lakri
kelema	sokhan ; lafz	lafz
shughl	kar	kam
sanayi	kargeramaley	karigar ; mazdur
arda	bad–tar	ziada kh'rab
abada ; sala	ibadat	ibadat ; puja
jurh	zakhm	zakhm
lef	band–	band– ; lapet-
keteb	navis	likh–
ghalat	ghalati	galat
sena	sal	sal ; baras
asfar	zard	pila
ey ; na'am	bale	han
embareh ; ems	diruz	kal
enta	shuma ; ghorban	ap ; tum
sughair	javan	jawan
–ek ; –kum	–atan	apka ; tumar'

TURKISH

Notes :

PRONUNCIATION : The stress in most words is on the last syllable.

WORD ORDER : Verbs always take last place in a sentence. 'The' is omitted. 'A, an' is *bir*. A definite object always precedes the subject; thus 'you saw the man' becomes '(the) man you saw'.

PREPOSITIONS : As in English, these precede the noun; but 'of', 'in', 'with', 'from' and 'to' are translated by case-endings which are added to the noun; thus 'of the stone': *tash-in;* 'to the stone': *tash-a;* 'in the stone': *tash-da;* 'from the stone': *tash-dan;* 'with the stone': *tash-ley.*

VERBS : Add the following endings to the roots given in the word-lists to show tense, etc :

Root-*in* . .	command (e.g. 'Go!')
Root-*yor-im* .	present ('I am going')
Root-*r-im* . .	" "
Root-*me-im* . .	negative ('I don't go')
Root *di-im* . .	past ('I went')
Root-*ajak-im* .	future ('I will go')
Root-*mish* . .	past participle (e.g. 'eaten', 'beaten')
Root-*mak* . .	infinitive ('to go,' 'to eat')
Root-*n* (or *l*) *im* .	passive ('I am beaten')

Root–*abil–im*	.	can (' I can go ')
Root–*ame–im*	.	can't (' I can't go ')
Root–*mali–im*	.	must (' I must go ')

The present tense of the verb ' to be ' is as follows : ' I am ' : *im*. ' You are ' : *sinez*. ' He is,' ' she is,' or ' it is ' : *dir* (or *dur*). ' We are ' : *iz*. ' They are ' : *dirler*.

To form ' you go,' ' he goes,' ' we go,' ' they go,' etc., change *im* in the above list of endings to *siniz*, *dir*, *iz*, *dirler*.

There is no verb ' to have.' ' To have ' is translated thus :

I have a (book) : My a (book) there is : *benim bir* (*kitab*) *var dir*.

I have no (book) : My a (book) not is : *benim bir* (*kitab*) *yoq dir*.

I have the (book) : In me (book) is : *benda* (*kitab*) *dir*.

Plurals : Nouns form the plural by adding *ler* : *kedi* (cat), *kediler* (cats). Adjectives, as in English, do not change in the plural.

Forming Words : You can greatly increase your vocabulary by adding the following endings to words in the word-list :

–*e* (or *el*)	e.g.	*qan* (blood)	.	*qane* (bleed)
–ja (or –*je*)		*beyaz* (white)	.	*beyazja* (whitish)
–ji		*ekmek* (bread)	.	*ekmekji* (baker)
–jik		*ev* (house)	.	*evjik* (little house)
–*le* (or–*len*)		*gōz* (eye)	.	*gözle* (to watch)

–lesh	*eyi* (*good*)	*eyilesh* (to get better)
–li (or–*lu*)	*ry* (place)	. *yerli* (local, native)
–lik (or *luk*)	*gün* (day)	. *günluk* (daily)
–siz	*para* (cash)	. *parasiz* (penniless)

Many new verbs can also be formed by combining nouns or adjectives with the verbs *et–* (do, make), *ol–* (be), and *olun–* (become) : thus *azad* (free) : *azad et–* (liberate) ; *hasta* (ill) : *hasta ol–* (to be ill).

Most adjectives can be used as adverbs without change.

TURKISH

Special List :

Albania . . . albann
Albanian . . . arnavud
Aleppo . . . haleb
America . . . ameriqa
American . . . ameriqali
apple . . . elma
apricot . . . qayisi ; zerdali
Arab . . . . arab
Arabia . . . arabistan
attack . . . hüjüm

battalion . . . tabur
battle . . . müdareba

brigade . . . liva
brigadier . . . miri-liva
buffalo . . . jamus; manda
Bulgarian . . . bulghar

cabbage . . . lahana
cake . . . . qurabiye
camel. . . . jemel; üshtür
cannon . . . top
captain . . . yuzbashi
caravan . . . kervan; qafile
Caucasia . . . qafqasiya
cherries . . . kiraz
China . . . chin
Chinese . . . chini
Christian . . . khristyan; isave
Circassian . . . cherkes
come! . . . haide
colonel . . . miralai; qaimaqam
company (mily.) . . bölük
conquest . . . fet'
Constantinople . istambol
Crete . . . girid
Cyprus . . . qubrus

Damascus . . . sham
division (mily.) . . firqa
Dutch . . . filemeng

Egypt . . . misir
England . . . ingliz
English . . . inglizi

Europe . . .	avropa
European . . .	avropali
France . . .	fransiz
French . . .	fransizi
general (mily.) . .	sardar ; feriq
German . . .	alman
God forbid ! . .	mazallah
God forgive me ! .	estaghfirullah
God is good ! . .	allah kerim
good-bye . . .	hoshja qalin
grapes . . .	üzüm
holy (or Saint) . .	hazreti
Holy Prophet, The .	resulu ekrem
how long? (time) .	ne qadar vaqit?
I think (probably) .	allehem
ice-cream . . .	dondurma
if God wish . .	inshallah
India . . .	hindistan
Indian . . .	hind
it is (2) o'clock . .	sa'at (iki) dir
Italian . . .	talyan
Jerusalem . . .	qudus
Jewish . . .	yehudi
Kurdish . . .	kürd
let us go . . .	haiden
lieutenant . . .	mulazim evvel

(2nd-lieutenant : . . mulazim sani)
lime, lemon . . limon
loaf . . . . somun
Magyar . . . majar
major (mily.) . . binbashi
malaria . . . isitma
meat, fried . . qavurma
meat, roasted . . qizartma

never mind . ehemiyeti yoq
no good . . . avara
no, thank you . . ziade olsun
(it is too much)
nut . . . findiq

Palestine . . . filistin
pardon . . . afv
parrot . . . papaghan
peace be with you ! . salamun alekum
(the usual greeting)
peach . . . sheftali
pear . . . . armud
Persia . . . iran
Persian . . . irani ; ajem ; farisi
please . . . lutfen ; kerem et–
plum . . . . erik
pomegranate . . nar
private (mily.) . . nefer

Rumanian . . . rum
Russian . . . mosgof

secret	sirr ; gizli
sergeant	sira chavushu
Smyrna	izmir
Spanish	ispanyol
sugar-plum	shekerleme
Syria	suriya
thank God	elhamdullah
thanks !	eyvallah
thank you	teshekur ederim ; memnun
treacle	bekmez
Tripoli	tarablus
Turkish	turkiyali
Turkey	turkiya
Turkish delight	loqum
welcome !	hosh geldiniz
well done !	aferin
what's the matter ?	ne var ?
what time is it ?	sa'at qach dir ?
wheat (crushed)	yarma
wolf	qurd
women's quarters	harem

ARABIC

Notes :

Two forms of Arabic are given in the word-lists. Western Arabic is spoken in Egypt and northern Africa, Eastern Arabic in Syria, Iraq, and Arabia proper. There are, of course, numerous local variations in the many Arabic-speaking countries, but the main division of vocabulary and idiom is represented in the two forms given in this book.

WORD ORDER : In a simple sentence, the order is very similar to that of English. ' A, an ' is omitted. ' The ' is *el ;* when *el* is followed by a word beginning with *d*, *n*, *r*, *s*, *t*, or *z*, the *l* is replaced by a corresponding letter ; thus ' the man ' : *er ragil* (*er rejil*) ; ' the soap ' : *es sabun*. Adjectives come after nouns, and when a noun is preceded by 'the,' a second ' the ' is inserted between the noun and the adjective ; thus, ' the old book ' becomes ' the book the old,' *el kitab el qadim. El kitab qadim* would mean ' the book is old '.

PREPOSITIONS : These come before the noun ; when they end in a vowel and are followed by *el*, they merge into it ; thus, ' in ' is *fi* ; ' in the ' is ' *fil* '.

PLURALS : Many nouns have irregular plurals which can only be learnt individually, but others form the plural by adding *-in*, *-a* or -(*a*)*t*. Adjectives form their plural by adding *-in*.

VERBS: Arabic verbs have no root in the strict sense. They show their different tenses and persons by changing internally as well as adding prefixes and suffixes. In the word-lists verbs are given in the accepted basic form, which is the third person singular of the past tense. The regular verb is conjugated thus:—

Basic form: *katab* (he wrote)

Present:

I write	*aktib*
you write	*tiktib*
he writes	*yiktib*
we write	*niktib*
they write	*yiktibu(m)*

The Future is shown by placing *rah* in front of the Present forms, or simply by the Present forms alone.

Past:

I wrote	*katabt*
you wrote	*katabt*
he wrote	*katab*
we wrote	*katabna*
they wrote	*katabu(m)*

Imperative:

write!	*iktib*

Participles:

writing	*katib*
written	*maktub*

Negative:

he did not write	*ma katabish* or *mush katab*

(*ma . . . (i)sh* and *mush* can also be used with pronouns ; thus, *ma lish* (' not to me,' i.e. ' I don't have')

The verb ' to be ' is generally omitted.

Many verbs conjugate irregularly, and these must be learnt individually.

Most passive participles, are used as nouns. Thus, *maktub*, means ' written ' or ' a letter '.

ARABIC

Special List :

	WESTERN	EASTERN *
alabaster	marmar	
Alexandria	iskandaria	
America	amerika ; bilad el malakan	
American	amrikan ; malakan	
apple	tiffaha	tuffaha
apricot	mishmisha	mishmish
Arab (adjective)	'arabi ; 'arab	
Arab (man)	ibne 'arab	
Arab (horse)	husan 'arab	
Arabia	bilad el 'arab	
Arabic	'arabi	
banana	moza	
battalion	orta	
battle	waqa	muharaba

* NOTE : In this list the Eastern Arabic form is only given where it differs noticeably from the Western

	WESTERN	EASTERN
Bedouin .	badawi	
beer . .	bira	
beggar . .	shahat . .	mugeddi
cabbage .	kurumb . .	lahana
Cairo . .	masr . .	el qahira
caliph . .	khalifa	
camel . .	gamal . . .	jemel
camel-driver .	gam'mal .	jam'mal
canal . .	tira . .	tura
captain . .	yuzbashi . .	yozbashi
caravan . .	karwan	
chess . .	shatrang .	satranj
China(-ese) .	es sin ; sini .	sin ; chin
Christ . .	el masih	
Christian .	nusrani . .	nasrani ; masihi
colonel . .	miralai ; qaimaqam	
come here ! .	ta'ala hina .	
company (mily.)	buluk	
Copt . .	qibti (plural : iqbat)	
date (fruit) .	balah	
Damascus .	esh sham	
Damietta .	dumyat	
Delta, the	ed delta	
desert, a .	khala . .	chol ; barr
dragoman .	turguman .	turjuman
Egypt . .	masr	
(Upper Egypt .	es sa'id)	

	WESTERN	EASTERN
Egyptian	masri	
England	bilad el Ingliz	anglaterra
English	ingliz(i)	anglez(i)
eunuch	khasi	
Europe	bilad el efrang; uruba	uropa
European	efrangi; rubawi	farnji; uropawi
fanatic	mit'assab	muta'asib
fez cap	tarbush	
fig	tina	
flea	barghut	barguth
French	fransawi	
Friday	yom eg'guma	yom el juma
general (mily.)	qaid'am; mushir; fariq	
German	almani	allamani; jarmani
Germany	almanya	bilad el jarman; allamanya
Gibraltar	gebel tariq	jebel tariq
gipsy	ghagari	kawli
go away!	imshi	
God be praised!	el hamdulillah	
God bless you!	allah yibarik fik	
God preserve you!	allah yisallimak	
God provide for you! (used to dismiss a beggar)	allah yirzuqak	

	WESTERN	EASTERN
God willing!	insh'allah	
good-bye	salem aleykum; ma'es salama	sellem aleykum; fi aman illah
good evening; good night	leyltak sa'ida	
grapes . .	'inab . .	'anab
Greece . .	bilad er rum	bilad el yonan
Greek . .	rumi; egrigi	yonani
how are you?	izzeyak . .	kif el-hal
in the name of God!	bismillah	
Indian . .	bilad el hind	hindustan; el hind
Indian . .	hindi	
infidel . .	kafir	
Italian .	talyani . .	italiyani
Japan .	yaban	
Jerusalem .	el quds	
Jew . .	yahudi	
Koran, the .	el quran	
lemon . .	limun	
Levant . .	esh sharq el aqrab	
lieutenant .	mulazim	
loaf . .	righif . .	samuna

	WESTERN	EASTERN
matter, it doesn't	ma'aleysh	
major (mily.)	binbashi	
matter, what's the	el khabar eh	esh aku
Mediterranean	el bahr el abyad	el bahr el mutawassit
minaret .	madna .	manara
Mohammedan, Moslem	muslim	
Moor . .	maghrabi	
Morocco .	marakish	
pardon . .	ef afw'	
peach . .	khokha	
peace be with you !	salam aleykum	sellem aleykum
peasant . .	fallah	
Persia . .	bilad el agam	bilad el ajem; iran
Persian . .	agami . .	ajemi ; irani ; farsi
please . .	min fadlak .	min fadlek
Pharaoh . .	fara'un	
pilgrim . .	hagg . .	haji ; zayir
piastre . .	qirsh . .	qursh
pound (20s.) .	gineh . .	pawn ; lira
prophet . .	nabi ; resul .	nebi ; resul
pyramid .	haram . .	herem
regiment .	tabur	

	WESTERN	EASTERN
Rosetta	rashid	
Russia	bilad el miskof	rusia
Russian	miskofi	rusi ; muskofi
sacred	muqaddas	
scarab	gu'ran	ju'ran
scorpion	aqraba	aqrab
sergeant	shawish	chawush
slave	abd	
sphinx	abul hol	
Sudanese	sudani	
sultan	sultan	
Syria	esh sham	sham ; suria
Syrian	shami	suri
thank you	katar kherak	mimnun ; muteshekker ; ket'ter khairek
Tripoli	trablis el gharb	
Turk(-ish)	turk(i)	turki ; osmanli
Turkey	bilad et turk	turkia
welcome !	ahlan wa sahlan	

PERSIAN

Notes :

PRONUNCIATION : The stress in most words is on the last syllable.

WORD ORDER : Verbs always take last place in a sentence. 'The' is omitted. 'A, an' is either *yek*, placed before a noun, or the ending *-i* added to it : thus, 'a book' can be *yek kitab* or *kitab-i*. Adjectives follow the nouns they belong to, and *-i-* is inserted between noun and adjective; thus, 'big book' *kitab-i-buzurg*. In translating a phrase including 'of', the English order is used; thus, 'the book of the child' is *kitab-i-bacha*. 'The child's big book' would be *kitab-i-buzurg-i-bacha*.

PREPOSITIONS : As in English, these precede the noun.

VERBS : The following prefixes and endings are added to the roots given in the word-lists to show tense, etc :—

be–Root–*id*	.	command (e.g. 'Go!')
mi–Root–*am*	.	present ('I am going')
Root–(*i*)*d*–*am*	.	past ('I went')
Root–(*i*)*dan*	.	infinitive ('to go')

The present tense of the verb 'to be' is as follows :—

'I am' *am*

'You are' *id*
'He is,' 'she is,' or 'it is' *ast*
'We are' *im*
'They are' *and*

To form 'you go,' 'we go,' 'they go' etc., change *am* in the list of endings given above to *id*, *im*, *and*. (*Ast* is not used as a verb ending; 'he goes,' 'he went' and similar forms are simply *mi*–Root, Root–(*i*)*d*). The future tense of verbs is identical with the present.

PLURALS: Nouns form the plural by adding *-ha*. Adjectives, as in English, do not change in the plural.

FORMING WORDS: You can increase your vocabulary by adding the following endings to words in the word-lists :—

–a	e.g. *garm* (hot) .	*garma* (heat)
–ban	*bagh* (garden)	*baghban* (gardener)
–i	*khub* (good) .	*khubi* (goodness)
–i	*Isfahan* .	*Isfahani* (of Isfahan)
–in	*shir* (milk) .	*shirin* (sweet)
–istan	*gul* (flower) .	*gulistan* (garden)
–var	*umid* (hope) .	*umidvar* (hopeful)

Many new verbs can also be formed by combining nouns or adjectives with the verbs *kun-* (do, make) and *shau-* (become); thus *safar kun-* (make a journey, i.e. travel); *kharab kun-* (make bad, i.e. spoil, damage); *kharab shau-* (become bad, i.e. be spoilt). The passive of any verb can also be formed as follows: Root – (*i*)*da* followed by *shau-* with the appropriate ending.

Most adjectives and many nouns can be used as adverbs: thus, *zud* (quick, or quickly); *shab* (night, or: at night).

PERSIAN

Special List:

America . . .	amrika
apple . . .	sib
apricot . . .	zardalu
Arab . . .	'arab
Arabia	arabistan
artillery . . .	topkhana
attack . . .	hamala
battalion . . .	gerdan
be careful! . .	khabar dar
beer . . .	ab–i–jo
beard . . .	rish
brigade . . .	tip
camel . . .	shutur
captain . . .	sarvan
Caspian Sea . .	bahr–i–khazar
Caucasus . . .	kuh–i–qaf; qafqaz
cellar (used as a living-room in hot weather)	sardab
cherry . . .	gilas; alubalu
China . . .	chin
Christian . . .	isavi
colonel . . .	sarhang
company (mily.) .	gerdan

date . . .	khorma
date-spirit . .	araq
Egypt . . .	mesr
England . .	inglestan
English . . .	inglis
Europe . . .	farangistan
European . .	farangi
excuse me . .	bebakhshid
fig . . .	anjir
France . . .	feransa
general (mily.) . .	sartip
Germany . . .	almanya
good-bye . . .	khuda hafiz
good-day . . .	shadzi
grapes . . .	angur
Greece . . .	yunan
headman . . .	kadkhoda
how long ? (time) .	ta ke
I don't know . .	namidanam
if God wills . . (i.e. perhaps)	inshallah
in the name of God !	bismillah
India . . .	hindustan
Iran . . .	iran
Iranian . . .	irani ; farsi
It is (2) o'clock .	sa'at–i–(do) ast
jackal . . .	shaghal

Japan . . .	zhapan
kerosene . . .	naft
lemon . . .	limu
lieutenant . . .	setvan
lizard . . .	bozmaja
loaf . . .	nan
locust . . .	malakh
major (mily.) . .	sargerd
meat, roasted on skewers	kabab
meat, boiled with rice	pilao
melon . . .	hendovana
melon, water . .	kharbuza
never mind . .	eb nist
nightingale . .	bulbul
n.c.o. . . .	goruhban
nut . . .	joz ; fondogh
oil . . .	naft
pace (20 ins.) . .	ghadam
peace be with you! (the usual greeting)	salam alekum
peach . . .	holu
pear . . .	golabi
Persia . . .	iran
Persian . . .	irani ; farsi
please . . .	be-farma-id
plum . . .	alu

pomegranate . .	anar
Russia . . .	rusya
saint . . .	pir
scorpion . . .	agharb
shrine . . .	ziyarat
sour milk, thickened	mast
spirit made from date-palm	araq
sheepskin coat . .	pustin
thank God! . .	elhamdullah
thank you . .	mamnun; motashakkar
Turkey . . .	torkiya
vulture . . .	kargas
water-pipe . .	qalyan
well done! . .	aferin; bakh bakh
what is the time? .	sa'at chand ast
what's the matter? .	in che chiz ast
wolf . . .	gurg
women's quarters .	andarun

HINDUSTANI

Notes :

PRONUNCIATION : When a consonant is followed by an apostrophe indicating a 'swallowed-sound,' this often indicates a very light aspirate, which in popular speech is generally omitted, or reduced to a mere catch in the voice.

WORD ORDER : The verb always comes at the end of a sentence. 'A, an,' and 'the' are omitted; but *ek* (one) is sometimes used where in English we would use 'a'. Adjectives precede nouns. Prepositions (properly called postpositions) follow the nouns they apply to, and in a phrase such as 'the brother of Krishna' the order is 'Krishna: of: brother' (*Krishna ka b'ai*); this corresponds to the English use of 'Krishna's brother.'

VERBS : Add the following suffixes to the roots given in the word-lists to show the various tenses :—

–t' .	Present (e.g. eats, is eating, am eating, are eating)
–' or *–a* .	Past (ate, was or were eating)
–'g' .	Future (will eat)
–o .	Command (eat !)
–ie .	Request (please eat)

'I am' is *main hun* ; 'you are,' *ap hain* (less politely, *tum ho*) ; 'he, she or it is,' *wuh hai* (*he*) ; 'they are,' *wuh hain*.

WORD FORMING: Verbs can be formed from most nouns by adding the verb *kar-* (do, make); thus, *safar* (journey): *safar kar-* (travel).

HAVE: There is no equivalent verb for 'have' in Hindustani. 'Krishna has X' is expressed by 'X is near Krishna;' the Hindustani order being 'X: Krishna: near is' : (*X Krishna k' pas hai*). When a pronoun is used in such a phrase, *k'* is omitted, and instead of 'I,' 'you,' 'he,' 'she,' 'we,' etc. the possessives 'my' 'your,' 'our,' etc. are used; thus, 'we have a dog' becomes 'dog: our: near (*pas*); is' (*kutta hamar' pas hai*).

HINDUSTANI

Special List:

alligator . . .	mag'r
areca-nut . . .	pan
attendant, orderly .	chaprassi
banana . . .	kela
basil (plant) . .	tulsi
basin . . .	chilamchi
be careful! . .	khabardar
betel-nut . . .	(*see* areca)
bird similar to starling	maina
boatman . . .	manji
brave . . .	b'hadur
butler . . .	abdar
butter, clarified .	g'i

camel . . .	unt
canal . . .	nahr
canopy . . .	pandal
cantonment . .	ch'aoni
charm, sacred formula (H)	mantra
China . . .	chin
cobbler . . .	mochi
court, assembly .	darbar
crocodile . . .	mag'r
crown . . .	taj
curry . . .	tarkari
custom . . .	dastur
deed, agreement .	sanad
deer (large) . .	sambur
doorkeeper . .	darwan
elephant . . .	hat'i
emperor . . .	badshah
England, the West, Europe	bilayat
England . . .	inglistan
English . . .	angrezi
fair (religious) . .	mela
fez cap . . .	tarbush
fish: white, river-fish	hilsa
similar to salmon	mahsir
food: meat cooked on small spits	kabab
pancake of unleavened bread	ch'patti

food: sweetened pancake	puri ; p'ratta
rice, meat, etc, fried together	pilao
sweets, confectionery, etc.	halwa
split peas, pulse, lentils, etc.	d'al
gardener . . .	mali
greetings: . .	salaam ; ram ram (H) ; namaste (H) ; salaam aleykum (M) ; sat s'ri akal (S)
gully, dry watercourse	nala
headman . . .	lambardar
hermit . . .	sanyasi (H)
India . . .	hind ; hindustan
it is (2) o'clock .	(do) baje he
jackal . . .	shaghal
known . .	malum
know, I don't . .	malum ney
landing-place . .	g'at
landowner . .	zamindar
lemon, lime . .	nimbu
lemonade . .	nimbu pani

loin-cloth, draped low	d'oti (H)
mail, post . .	dak
made in India . .	swadeshi
mango . . .	am
melon . . .	kharbuza
mendicant (religious) .	sad'u (H) ; faqir (M)
merchant . . .	mahajan ; bania
molasses, coarse sugar	gur
monsoon, the rains .	barsat
morning tea . .	chota hazri
mosquito . .	mach'r
mosquito-net . .	mach'rdani
pilgrim . . .	haji (M)
Persian . . .	farsi ; irani
pipe, for smoking through water .	huqa
pith (helmet) . .	sola (topi)
platform built as stand for hunter . .	machan
pony-trap . . .	tanga
precipice . . .	k'ad
preacher . . .	mulla ; maulvi (M)
ranks :	
Viceroy's Commissioned Officers : . .	risaldar subadar jemadar
sergeant . .	havildar
corporal . .	naik

regiment . . .	paltan ; risala (cavalry)
rogue . . .	badmash
Russia(n) . . .	rus(i)
saint . . .	pir (M)
scullery-boy (originally torch-bearer) .	masalchi
self-government .	swaraj
servant . . .	naukar
show, entertainment .	tamasha
staff, pole . . .	lat'i
stone blockhouse .	sangar
strike, a . . .	hartal
sweeper . . .	mehtar
tanner . . .	chamar
teacher (of law, religion etc.) . . .	pandit (H) ; munshi, maulvi (M) ; guru (S & H)
thank you . .	mirbani ; shukria
tiger . . .	bag'
tip, alms . . .	bakshish
titles :	
leader . . .	sardar (S)
lion . . .	singh (S & H)
lord . . .	khan (M)
prince . . .	rana ; rao ; rai (H)
trees :	
ficus indica (banyan) . .	bar
ficus religiosa (peepul ; bo) . .	pipal

trees : azadirachta indica (neem)	nim
trooper . . .	sowar
veranda . . .	baramda
village council . .	panchayat
water-man . .	b'ishti
water-skin . .	chagal
water-tank, portable .	pakal
well done ! . .	shabash
what's the matter ? .	kya bat he
what's the time ? .	kitna baje he
white man . .	gora
wise man . . .	mantri
women's quarters .	zenana

NOTE : (H), (M), and (S) indicate words used by Hindus, Muslims and Sikhs respectively.

Part Two

JAPANESE

CHINESE (MANDARIN)

CHINESE (CANTONESE)

SIAMESE

BURMESE

ENGLISH	JAPANESE	CHINESE (M.)
above	kami	shang–to
absent	rusu	bu dzai
accident	wazawai	shi–shan
address	shuku–sho	ju–jö
after	nochi ; go	liau–ho
afternoon	hiru–sugi ; gogo	ho ban dien
again	mata	dzai
age	toshi ; nenrey	nien–ji
alive	ikite	hwaw
all	mina	do ; van
all right	yoshi	hau–la
allow	yurus–	rang
alone	hitori	dan
also	mo ; yahari	yeh
always	mai–do	jang jang
and	to	hö
angry	haratachi	shang chi
animal	dobutsu	chu shang
ant	ari	ma–i
anything	nan de mo	dung shi
are	(arimas' ; des')	—
arm	ude ; te	go pey
army	rikugun	lu jün
around	gururi	go bien
arrangement	yakusoku ; kimari	ban va
arrive	chaku sur–	dau
ask	kik– ; tanom–	wan ; yau
at	–ni	dzai

CHINESE (C.)	SIAMESE	BURMESE
tzoi–song	k'ang–bon	a–tet–ma
m'tzoi	mai–yu	ma–yauk
si pin	aksiden	pyit–chin
tey-po	ti-yu	ma–za–leyk
yi hau	k'ang–lang	nauk–ma
ha chau	weyla bai	mun–lwe a–cheyn
tzoi	ik ti	ta–pan
nin key	ayu	a–thet–a–yue
sang–tik	ahkat	a–that–shi–thaw
yat–chai	tang–mot	a–lon
ho	tok–long	kaung–ba–byi
chun	yawm	a–kwin pey
tok	dio	ko di
yik	duey	li
si si	samö	a–mye
tung	le	hnin
nau hey	krot	a–myet
kam sau	sat	tha
ma–ngai	mot	pa–yuet–seyt
yong yong	arai	ta–zon–ta–khu
—	pen	pyit
sau pey	k'an	let–maung
lok kwan	kong tap	thu–ye–dat–su–ji
si wai	rawb	pat–le
pai lik	kan chat kan	thabaw–du–sa–jok
tau	tüng	yauk
man ; man sün	tam ; k'aw	mey ; taung
tzoi	ti	ma ; ni

ENGLISH	JAPANESE	CHINESE (M.)
back (noun)	ushiro ; senaka	ho bey
bad	warui ; aku	bu hau
bag	fukuro	ko tai
bandage	hotai	bu
barber	kami–yiu	di do va ta
basket	kago	kuang dzö
bath (tub)	furo–ba	pan
bathe	mizu wo abir–	shi dzau
bathroom	furo–ba	shi dzau wu
be	(ar– ; ir–)	—
beans	mame	do dzö
beautiful	uruwashii	hau kan
because	kara	yin wey
become	nar–	chang
bed	nedoko	chwang
bedroom	nema ; nebeya	wo vang
before (time)	mai ; –zen	chien to
begin	hajimer–	chi lai
behind	–no kage ni	ho to
bell	kane	ling dang
below	shimo	di shia
bench	seki	i dzö
best	mottomo ii	dzui hau
between	–no naka ni	dzai jung jien
big	okii ; dai	da
bill (check)	kanjo	jing dan
bird	tori	niau ö
black	kuroi	hey
blacksmith	tekko	tieh jang
blanket	furanketto	jan dzö

CHINESE (C.)	SIAMESE	BURMESE
pui	lang	chaw–gon
m'ho ; ok	leo ; chua	ma kaung ; so
toi	ka–pao	lwe–ait
pong po	pa pan pla	chat–si–ya
fey fat lo	chang tat pom	satta–the
lam	ka-chat ; ka–chao	thaung
chung lŏng pun	tang na	mwe–thi
sai san	ap nam	yey–cho
chung lŏng fong	hong nam	yey–cho–gan
—	pen	pyit
tau	tua	pe
mey lai	ngam ; suey	hla
yan wai	praw wa	jaung
sing	pen	pyit; pyit–lo–thi
chong	tiang	ka–din
fan fong	hong–nawn	eyk–ya–gan
yi chin	kawn	a–yin–ga
hoi sau	röm	a–sa–pyu
hau pin	k'ang lang	nauk–ma
chung	krading	si–li
ha tai	k'ang lang	auk–ma
chong tang	ma nang	thai–khun–shi
chui ho	di ti sut	a–kaung–son
kang ku chü	rawang	sat–cha–ma
tai	yai	chi ; ji
chong muk	bill	sa–yin
chök	nok	nget
hak	dam	me
ta tit chong	chang lek	pa–be
chin	pa hom	saung

ENGLISH	JAPANESE	CHINESE (M.)
blood	chi	shieh
blue	aoi	lan
board	tana	ban dzö
boat	kobune	jwan
boil, to	wak– ; nir–	ju
bone	hone	gu do
book	hon ; shomotsu	shu
boot	kutau	shüeh dzö
born, to be	umare–	shang
box	hako	shiang dzö
boy	musuko	hai dzö
brass	shinchu	tung
bread	pan	mien bau
break, to	or–	ta paw
bribe, a	naimai	hui lu
brick	renga	jwan to
bridge	hashi	chiau
brother	ue	gaw gaw
brush, a	hoki	shwa dzö
build	tater–	gai
building, a	tatemono	vang wu
bullock	ushi	gung niu
burn, to	yak–	shau
bush	bara	dzau
business	gyo	shi
buy	ka–	mai
by	–ni	jin ; dzai
call	yob–	jiau

CHINESE (C.)	SIAMESE	BURMESE
hüt	lüet	thwey
lam sik	si nam ngön ; si fa	a–pya
pan	kra–dan	pyin
sam–pan	rüa	tham–pan
kwan	tom	pyok–thi
kwat	kra duk	a–yo
sü	nang süa	sa–ok
hai	rong tao	but–p'nat
chut sai	köt	mwe–pwa–thi
siong	hib	thit–ta
nam tzi	dek pu chai	lu–galey
tung	tong lüang	chey–wa
min pau	k'anom pang	mon
ta lan	hak ; tamtak	cho
fui kok	sin bon	a–ku–sa–thi
chün	it	ok
kiu	sapan	ta-da
hing tey	pi chai ; nong chai	nyi
chat	prang	wet–min–bi
hey	sang ; s'rang	sauk
uk	tük	a–saung
ngau	ngua ; wua	na–ti
siu	pao	mi laung
chong lam	pum mai	chon
sang yi	ngan ; kam	a–lok–a–kin
mai	sü	we
kan pey	döi	pyin
kiu	tam ha	kaw ; laik

ENGLISH	JAPANESE	CHINESE (M.)
camp	ya'ey	ying pan
can	dekimas	de
cannot	dekimasen	bu de
candle	rosoku	la
cane	tsue	tang dzö
carpenter	daiku	mu jiang
carpet	shiki-mono	tan dzö
carriage	basha	che
cart	basha	ma che
cat	neko	mau
catch, to	tera'er-	jieh chiu
cave	ana	dung dzö
ceiling	tenjo	dien hwa ban
chain	kusari	saw lien dzö
chair	isu	i dzö
change, to	kawar-	hwan
check (bill)	kanjo	jing dan
chief	kashira	torö
child	ko	hai dzö
choose	erab-	tiau
church	kyokwaido	jiau dang
cigarette	maki-tabako	yen ju'ŏ
city	tokai	chang
clean	kirey	gan jing
clerk	shoki	shu ban
climb	nobor-	dang gau
clock	tokey	piau
cloth	kire	bu
clothes	kimono	i-shang
cloud	kumo	yün

CHINESE (C.)	SIAMESE	BURMESE
kwan ying	k'ai	sa–kan
nang	dai	nin
m'cho tak	mai dai	ma–nin–bu
lap chuk	tian	pa–yaung–ding
tang	mai ; wai	dok
muk chiong	chang mai	let–tha–ma
te tzin	süa	kaw–zaw
che	rot	ya–ta
che	kwian	le
mau	meo	chaung
chuk	chap	pan–zi
san ngam	tam	ku
uk löng	pedan	myet–na–jet
ti lin	so	cho–ji
yi tang	kao	ka–la–ting
wun	plian	pyaung
chong muk	bill	sa–yin
tau	hua na	tik th'ji
sai man tzai	dek	ka–ley
kan	lüek ; luk	ywe–thi
lai pai tong	rong suat	thudamma–za–yat
yin	buri	sey–leyk
seng	müang ; nakon	myo
ching key	sa'at	sin
si ma yün	samian	sa–yey
pan	pin	tet
chung	nalika	mat–tat na–yi
po	pa	tha–ga–lat
i–söng	süa pa	a–wut
wan	mek	mo–dey

ENGLISH	JAPANESE	CHINESE (M.)
coat	uwagi	gwa dzö
cock	on–dori	gung ji
coffee	kohi	ga vey
cold	samui ; tsumetai	lang
collar	kara	ling dzö
comb	kushi	mu shu
come, to	kuk– ; mair–	lai
concerning	–ni tsuite	go bien
cook, a	ryori–nin	chu dzö
cook, to	ryori sur– ; tak–	ju
corner	kado ; sumi	ji jiau ö
correct	honto	dui law
cost (noun)	ne dan	jia chien
cotton	momen	mien hwa
count	kazoer–	paw jüeh
country	shu ; kuni	gwaw
courtyard	niwa	yuen dzö
cover, to	shimer–	gai shang
cow	ushi	mu niu
crowd	ozey	da cha
cup	wan	bey
cupboard	todana	wan ju
curtain	maku	jang dzö
cushion	makura	dien dzö
cut, to	kir–	la
daily	nichi nichi	tien tien
damage	kizu ; itami	sun
dance, to	odor–	tiau wu

CHINESE (C.)	SIAMESE	BURMESE
sam	süa	in–ji
kai kung	kai tua pu	chet–pa
ka fe	kafa	ka–pi
lang	nao	ey-jin
leng	plawk kaw	le-bat
saw	wi	bi
loi	ma	la
kwan yü	kio ka	sing yuey
choi tzi	k'on k'rua	o–thu–ji
chü	tam k'rua	chet
kok	mum ; hua lio	daung
chök	tuk	hok
ka chin	kha	a–po
min fa	fai ; samli	waw–jun
sün	nap	ywi
kwok	patet ; pen din	chi–daw
ting cheng	suan	u–yin
kam	k'lum	ok
ngau	wua	nwa–ma
taw yin	mu ; kawng	lu–su
pui	tuey	kwet
kwai	tu	thit–ta
lim	man	ka–la–ga
yu tzam	mawn	mi–on
kawt	tat	kok
yat yat	tuk wan	ney–zin
sun sat	kwan sia–hai	a–cho–pyet–chin
tiu mo	ten ram	ka

ENGLISH	JAPANESE	CHINESE (M.)
danger	kennon	shien
dark	kurai	va hey
date (day)	nichi	ji dzö
daughter	musume	gun yang
dawn	yo-ake	li ming
day	nichi	tien
dead	naku	sö law
dear (cost)	takai	guey
deep	fukai	shan
die	naku nar–	wang
difficult	muzukashii	nan
dig	hor–	pau
dinner	hiru	wan van
dirty	kitanai	ang dzang
dish	ozara	pan dzö
district	kinjo	shien
do	sur– ; nas–	dzaw
don't !	– inasanna	bey–
doctor	isha	i sheng
dog	inu	go
donkey	roba	lü
door	to	man
down	sh'ta	shia
drain	umedoyu	go
dress, a	kimono ; ifuku	vu ran shan
drink, to	nom–	haw
drive, to	basha nor–	je vu

CHINESE (C.)	SIAMESE	BURMESE
ngai him	kwan antarai	be
ye hak	müd ; si–ke	nyo
yat tzi	wan ti	ney–zwe
nöi	butri	thami
ley ming	yam rung ; rung chao	mo–lin–za
yat	wan	ney ; yet
si	tai	they–bi
kwai	peng	a–po–chi
sam	lük	net
si	tai	they
nan	yak	ke
wat	k'ud	tu
man chan	ahan yen	mun–lwe–za
wu cho	sok kaprok	nyit
tip	chan	pa–gan–bya–ji
tey fong	tambon ; changwat	tik ; ne
cho	tam	pyu ; lok
pat yu–	ya	ma – – ne
yi sang	maw	sey–sya ; sey–thama
kau	sunak	kwey
löi	la	mye
mun	pratu	ta–ga
ha	long	auk–tho
köi	tam hai hang	myaung
yi sam	krüang tang tua	ga–ga–ya
yam	düm	thauk
cha che	k'ap ; lai	pyaw

ENGLISH	JAPANESE	CHINESE (M.)
drop (let fall)	otos–	diau shia chü
duck	ahiru	ya dzö
dust	gomi	chan tu
each	zutsu ; mai	mey
east	higashi	dung
easy	yasui ; yo–i	jung i
eat	taber–	chi
egg	tamago	(ji) dan
eight	hachi ; ya	ba (gaw)
eleven	ju-ichi ; ju-itto	shi i (gaw)
empty	kara	kung
end	sue ; owari	wan ; we
enemy	teki	cho ren
enough	takusan na ; buri	go
enter	(ha–)ir–	jin
envelope	jobukuro	vang tau ö
evening	ban	wan shang
explain	tok–	jiang
extinguish	kes–	mieh
extra	hijo	ja'i gö
eye	me	yen jing
face	kao	mien mau
fall, to	ocnir–	shi wey
family	saishi	jia
fan	uchiwa	shan dzö
far	toi	yuan gaw
farmer	hyakusho	dien hu

CHINESE (C.)	SIAMESE	BURMESE
lok ha	tam tok	lut
ap	pet	wumbe
chan	fun	pon
möi	tuk ; la	–si
tung	tit t'wan awk	a–shey
yung yi	ngai	lwe
sik	kin	sa
tan	k'ai	chet u
pat	pat	shit
sap yat	sip et	se ta
hung	wang	lut–lat
mey ; cho yün	plai ; lao	a–son
tik yen	satru	yan–thu
chuk	paw lao	lauk ; taw
yap	k'ao	win
son fung	sawng	sa–eyk
ai man	(weyla) yen	nya–ney
kai	atibai	pya
mit	dap	nying–thi
yü ngoi	piset	lun
ngan	ta	myet–si
men (min)	na	myet–na
tit lok	tok	cha
ka	krawb krua	a–myo–a–nwe
sin	pat	yat–taung
yün	klai	wey
nung fu	chao no	le–lok–thama

ENGLISH	JAPANESE	CHINESE (M.)
fasten	shimer–	gün
fat (stout)	futotta	vey
father	otosan ; gosompu	vu chin
fear, to	osorer–	pa
feast	matsuri ; gochiso	shi
feed, to	tabesaser–	wey
female	mesu	mu di
fence	hey	li ba
fetch	motte kur–	na lai
fever	netsu	jaw bing
few	sukunai	shau
field	hatake ; nohara	tien di
fight, to	tataka–	da jia
find, to	hiro–	dzau
finger	yubi	ji to
finish	sum–	wan
fire	hi	hwaw
first	dai ichi	to i gaw
fish	sakana ; uwo	yü
five	go ; itsu	wu gaw
flag	hata	chi dzö
flat	taira	ping
flood	de-midzu	sha shue
floor	yuka	di ban
flour	kona	bai mien
flower, a	hana	hwa
fly, a	hai	tsang ying
fog	kiri	wu

CHINESE (C.)	SIAMESE	BURMESE
kau	mat	lon–chon
fey	au–en	tok
fu	bida ; paw	a–pey
pa	klua	so–yeyn–jin
yin chan	ngan kin liang	pwe–ney
wai	ha ahan	chwe
nöi sing	pu ying	meyn–ma
li pa	rua ; kawk	win
ning	pai ao ; song	yu–la
fat siu peng	kai	pya–na
siu	noi	ne
tin	rai ; tung na	le–ya
ta kau	taw su	sit–tik–thi
wan	ha	twey
sau tsi	ni mü	let–chaung
cho yün	set	a–sa–that
faw	fai	mi
tai yet	ti nüng	pa–ta–ma
yü	pla	nga
ng'	ha	nga
key	tong	a–lan
peng	ban	pya
söi cham	nam tuam	yey–det
lau pan	pün	chan
min fan	pang sali	mon-nyet
fa	dok mai	pan
u ying	maleng wan	yin–gaung
en mo	mawk	nin

ENGLISH	JAPANESE	CHINESE (M.)
fold, to	or–	dieh
follow	tsug–	ho ben
food	tabemono ; gohan	chi shi
foot	ashi	jiau
for (prep.)	no	gey
foreigner	gwaikoku-jin	wai gwaw ren
forest	hayashi	shu lin
forget	wasurer–	wang ji
fork	hoko	cha dzö
fort	shiro	bau dai
four	shi ; yo(–tsu)	sö (gaw)
friend	tomodachi	pang yo
from	–kara	dzung ; ju
front, in	saki	chen do
fruit	kudamono	gwaw dzö
fry	abur–	ja
fuel	nenryo	bi jai
garden	niwa	yüan dzö
gate	mon	man
gather	atsumar–	jau ji
gentleman	shinshi	jün
get	er–	de
girl	musume ; onna no ko	nu hai ö
give	kurer– ; okur–	gey ; sung
glass (drinking)	koppu	baw li
glass (looking)	kagami	jing dzö

CHINESE (C.)	SIAMESE	BURMESE
chip	pap	khaut–thi
kan	tam	lik
sik mat	ahan	sa–zya
kiok	k'on ngo	chi
pey	samrap	bo
ngoi kwok yan	chao tang pratet	da brey tha
sü lam	pa ; kanon ; dong	taw
mong key	leyum	mey lyaw
cha	sawm	ka–yin
pau toi	pom (kai)	dok
si	si	ley
pang yau	puen	meyk–swey
yau	jak	ga
min chin	k'ang na	she
kwaw tzi	pon (–lamai)	thi
tzin	tawt	chaw–thi
yin liu	tan fai	chauk–mi–thwey
fa ün	suan	u–yin
mun	pratu	ta–ga
sau chap	kep	su–wey
sin sang	supara burut	th'kin
law	pai ao	ya
nöi tzai	dek pu ying	meyn–ka–ley
pey	hai	pey
paw le pöi	tuey keo	pan–ga–don
min keng	gra'chok	man

ENGLISH	JAPANESE	CHINESE (M.)
glove	tebukuro	sho tau
goat	yagi	shan yang
go	mair–	chü
god	tenshu ; kami	shang di
gold	kin	jin
good	ii ; yoi ; yoshi	hau
goods	shina (–mono)	ho wu
government	seyfu	jang vu
gown	kimono	vu ran shan
grain	ko-mugi	liang shi
grass	shiba	tsau
grave	haka	van
grease	abura	yu
great	okii ; dai	da
green	aoi ; midori	lu
greet	keyrey sur–	dau shi
ground	tsuchi	di
grow	sodats–	jang
guest	kyaku	ko ren
guide	annai	ling lu di
gun	ho ; teppo	chiang
hair	kami ; ke	mau
half	hambun	i ban
hand	te	sho
handkerchief	hanafuki	sho bu
handle	e ; te	sho pa
happen	arr– ; okor–	chang
happy	shiawase	shi hwan

CHINESE (C.)	SIAMESE	BURMESE
sau to	tung mü	let–sut
yöng	pa	seyt
höi	pai	thwa
söng tai	pra chau	pa–ya–th'kin
kam	tong	shwey
ho	di	kaung
faw mat	sin ka	pyit–se
ching fu	rataban	a–so–ya
po	süa klum	ga–ga–ya
kuk	mlet ; met kao	a–the–a–nan
cho	ya	myet–pin
fan mo	u mong ; lum fang sop	thin–jin
yau	nam man	si
tai	yai	chi ; ji
chang	si kio	seyn
fun ying	sadang kwam yindi	ma–ba–i–la
tey	din	myey
chöng tai	kün	to
hak	kak	a–ye–thi
höng to	kon nam tang	lan–bya
chöng	pün	yik–pat
fat	fom	sa-bin
yat pun	küng ; krüng	ta–wet
sau	mü	let
sau kan	pa chet na	let–king–ba–wa
pang	ti chap	ta–zai
pong to	göt kün	mi
fai lok	sabai	chan–tha

ENGLISH	JAPANESE	CHINESE (M.)
hat	boshi	mau dzö
he	ano shto	ta
head	kubi ; atama	nau dai
hear	kik–	ting
heart	shin	shin
heaven	ten	tien
heavy	omoi	jung
hedge	hey	li ba
hen	niwatori	mu ji
here	kochi ; koko ni	ja li
high	takai	gau
hill	yama	shan
hire, to	karir– ; yato–	gu
his	ano shto no	ta di
home	uchi ; taku	jia
home, at	o taku de	dzai jia
honest	shojiki	shi chang
honey	mitsu	vang mi
hope, to	kibo sur–	bang wang
horse	uma	ma
hospital	byo-in	jün
hot	atsui	nwan haw
hotel	yado	geh yö
hour	jikan	i dien jung
house	uchi; taku; ie	vang dzö
how ?	do	dzan maw
how much ?	ikahodo ; ikura	daw shau
hundred, a	hyaku	bai
hunt, to	rio sur–	jui

CHINESE (C.)	SIAMESE	BURMESE
mo	müek	tho-ok–tok
köi	kau	thu
tau	hua	ok–kaung
teng	dai yin	cha
sam	hua chai	nit–lon
tin	sawan ; fa	mo
chung	nak	ley
ley pa	rua ; rua ton mai	si–dan
kai na	ma kai	chet–ma
ni chü	ti ni	di–ma
ko	sung	myin
san	kao ; pukao	taung
cho	hai chao	nga
köi	kong kau	thu
ka	ban ; rüan	eyn
choi ka	tiban	eyn–nik
sing sat	sü trong	pyaung–mat
mat tong	nam püng	pya–yi
hey mong	wang	myaw–lin
ma	ma	myin
yi yün	rong p'yaban	thu–na–dan
yit	rawn	pu
löi tim	patakan ; hoten	tamin–zing
tim chung	chua mong	na–yi
ok	ban ; rüan	eyn ; tik
tim yöng	tao rai	be ne
key to	tao rai	be lauk
yat pak	roi	t–ya
ta lit	la	lik

ENGLISH	JAPANESE	CHINESE (M.)
hurt, to	itamer–	sun
husband	ottɔ ; teyshu	jang vu
hut	koya	dzau vang
I	wata(ku)shi	waw
if	naraba	jaw
ill	byoki	yu bing
immediately	jiki ; sugu	jan dzai
important	taishita	bi yau
ink	sumi	maw
inn	yado	lü gwan
insect	mushi	jung
interpreter	tsuben	tung i kwan
into	ye	li bien
iron	tetsu	tieh
is	(arimas'; da ; des')	(shi)
is not	arimasen	pu (shi)
island	shima ; jima	hai dau
it	are	ta
jewel	tama	sho shir
journey	ryoko ; tabi	lü shing
judge, a	saiban-nin	tsai pan kwan
jug	yakan	gwan dzu
jump, to	tob–	tiau gwaw chü
juice	shiru ; midzu	shui ö
kettle	tetsubin	shwe hu
key	kagi	yau shi
kick, to	ker–	ti
kill	koros–	sha

CHINESE (C.)	SIAMESE	BURMESE
ta söng	tam antarai	na chi
chong fu	sami	lin
pang	katawm	eyn–gok
ngaw	chan	ch'nok
yök	ta	lyin
peng	puey	na
lap hak	tanti	ta ka di
kan yu	samkan	ga–yu pyu–bwe
mak	mük	min–yi
hak chan	hoten	tamin–zing
chong	malang	po–gaung
fanyik yan	lam	sa–ga–byan
löi	nai	de–tho
tet	lek	than
(hai)	piu ; mi	—
m' (hai)	mai piu	ma– – –bu
to	ko	chun
ta	mau	to
po sak	krüang pet	ta–za
löi hang	kan dön tang	ka–yithwa
fat kun	popipaksa	taya–thuji
söi wu	yüak	ka–ya
tiu	kadot	kon
chap	nam lok mai	si
wu	ka nam	yey–nwey–o
saw si	luk kunchai	thaw
tek	tae	kan–the
shat	ka	that

ENGLISH	JAPANESE	CHINESE (M.)
kind (amiable)	shinsetsu na	shan
kind (sort)	shina ; shurui	yang dzö
king	o	gwaw hwang
kitchen	katte	chu vang
knife	hocho	shiau dau dzö
know, to	shir–;mitomer–	shau dö ; ren dö
lady	fujin	tang kaw
lake	kosui	hu
lamb	kohitsuji	gau yang
lamp	rampu	tang
land	riku	di
lane	michi	hu tung ö
language	kotoba	hwa
large	okii	da
last	suye no	dzui ho
late	osoi	wan
laugh, to	wara–	shiau
law	kisoku ; ho	va
lawyer	bengoshi	lü sör
lead, to	hik–	ling
leaf	ha	shu yeh dzö
learn	nara–	shüeh
leave (of absence)	itoma	gau jia
left (side)	hidari	dzaw
leg	ashi	tui
lend	kas-	chiö gey
less	motto sukunai	shau
letter	tegami	shin

CHINESE (C.)	SIAMESE	BURMESE
yau sam	chai di	nu–nyan
yöng	yang	a–mye
wong	prachao pandin	shin–ba–yin
chöi fong	hong kroa	ta–min–jet–yon
to	mud	da
chi to ; shik	ru ; ruchak ; trap	thi
nöi tzi	supap satri	th'kin–ma
wu	ta sap ; baw	in
yöng tzai	luk ka	nye–tho
tang	takieng	mi–eyn
tey	ti din ; bok	kon
hawng	krawk	lan
wa	pasa	pyaw–jin
tai	yai ; to	chi–che ; ji
chöi hau	ti sut	nauk–son
chi	sai	nauk–kya
siu	huaro	ye
fat löt	kot mai	ta–ya
löt si	tanai kwam	shey–ney
tai	nam (hna); song	lan–bya
yip	bai (mai)	a–yuet
hok	rien	thin
ko ka	la pak	a–kwin
chaw sau	sai (mü)	let–we–bet
kiok	k'a	chi–dauk
tsia	yüm	chi
siu	noi kwa	tet
sön	chot mai	ma–za

ENGLISH	JAPANESE	CHINESE (M.)
lie down	fuser–	dang
lift, to	mochi-ager–	jü chi lai
light, a	akari	ji gwang ö
light, to	tak–	dien
light (weight)	karui ; usui	chen
line	suji	dau
listen	kik–	ting
little, a	shosho ; sukoshi	shau
live	ikir–; sum–	ju
lock	jomae	saw
long (distance)	nagai	chang
lose	ushina–	sun hai
love	aisur–	ai
low	hikui	ai
madam	okusama	dai dai
make	sur–	dzaw
man	otoko	ren
many	taksan	daw
map	chizu	tu
market	ichi	shi
marriage	kon-in	shi shi
master	shu ; danna	dung jia
mat	tatami	shi
match	machi	yang ho
mattress	futon	jwang dan
me	wata(ku)shi ni	waw
meat	niku	jo
medicine	kusuri	yau
meet	ni a–	shiang hui

CHINESE (C.)	SIAMESE	BURMESE
fan ta'i	nawn long	eyk
koi	yok	chi
tang faw	daking	a–lin
tim	chut fai	tun
heng	bao	paw
sin	siu	cho–ji
teng	fang	na
taw siu	ta noi	ne ne
sang chün	yu	a–thet shin
saw	kunchai	thaw–eyn
chöng	yen ; klai	shey
sit	tam hai	shon
oi	rak	chit–chin
ta'i	tam	neyn
tai tai	nang	kadaw
cho	tam	pyu
yan	pu chai	yauk–ya
ho taw	lai	mya
tey to	pan ti	mye bon
kai si	talat	zey
fan yan	kan dang ngan	let–tat–chin
chü yan	nai hang	th'kin
tsek	süa	pya
faw chai	mai kit fai	mi–jit
söi yuk	tiang	mi–jey–ya
ngaw	chan	ch'nok
yuk	nüa	a–tha
yök	ya	sey–wa
kin	pop	twey–chon

ENGLISH	JAPANESE	CHINESE (M.)
meeting	kwai	hui
mend	naos–	jin bu
merchant	akindo ; shonin	shang ren
midnight	yonaka	ban yeh
milk	chichi	niu nai
minute	fun	i van jang
mistake	chigai	tsaw law
money	kin ; kane	chien
monkey	saru	ho dzö
month	getsu ; tsuki	yüeh
moon	tsuki	yüeh
more	mo(–tto) ; nao	daw
morning	asa	dzau chi
mosque	kaikyo jiin	höi höi dang
most	ichi–ban	ding
mother	okkasan ; gobodo	mu chin
motor-car	jidosha	ji jo
mountain	yama ; –san	shan
mouth	kuchi	dzui
move, to	ugok–	dung
Mr.	san	shien sang
Mrs.	sama	dai dai
much	yohodo ; takusan	tai daw
mud	doro	ni
mule	raba	lo dzö
music	ongaku	yüeh
my	wata(ku)shi no	waw di
nail (iron)	kugi	ding dzö

CHINESE (C.)	SIAMESE	BURMESE
kin min	kan pop	twey–chon–thi
po	ka	pyin–zin
söng yan	k'on kai kong	sing–the
pun ye	weyla ting kün	tha–gaung
nai	nom ; nam nom	na–no
fan	nati	minit
chaw	sing ti pit	a–mo
ngan	ngön	nwe
hau	ling	myauk
yüt	düan	la
yüt	prachau	la
taw	ik	on ; the
cho san	(weyla) chao	ma–net
miu	wat ; bost' kek	mosjid
taw so	ti sat	a–zon
mo chan	mama	a–mey
hey che	rot-yon	ma–taw ta–sa
san	(pu)kao	taung-ji
hau	pak	pa–zat
yuk	pai	shwey
sin sang	nai	kin–bya
fu yan	nang	th'kin–ma
ho taw	mak	mya–zua
nai	klon	shun
loi	la	mye
yam ngawk	pleng	bun
ngaw ke	kong chan	ch'nok
teng	tapu	twe–at

ENGLISH	JAPANESE	CHINESE (M.)
name	na(–mai)	shing
narrow	semai	jai
nation	koku–jin	gwaw jia
near	chikai	jin
nearly	hotondo	cha i dien
necessary	iriyo	bi yau
needle	hari ; nuibari	jan
never	itsu mo– –en	lau bu
new	shin ; atarashii	shin
news	shimbun	shin wan
newspaper	shimbun (–shi)	shin wan bau
next	tsugi	ja i go
night	yo (–ru)	yeh
nine	ku ; kokono (–ts)	jiu gaw
no	iiye	bu jieh
noon	shogo ; hiru	shang wu
north	kita	bey
nose	hana	bi dzu
not	–en ; nai	bu ; mey
nothing	nani mo– –en	mey yu
now	ima	shien dzai
number	kazu ; su	dzö
o'clock	–ji	dien jung
of	–no ; teki	(–ti)
office	jimusho	jü
officer	shoko ; shikwan	wu gwan
often	yoku	chang
oil	abura	yu
O.K. (all right)	yoshi	hau la
old	furui	lau

CHINESE (C.)	SIAMESE	BURMESE
sing ming	chü	a-myi
chak	kap	pa
kwok ka	chati	pyi–thu
kan	klai	ni
chöng kan	küap	lu
pit sui	cham pen	ga–yu pyu–bwe
cham	kem	at
wing pat	mai– –löi	ta–ka–mya–ma
san	mai	thit
san man	k'ao	thadin
po tsi	nangsü pim	thadin sa
key chi	tat pai	a–ni–zon
ye man	(weyla) lang kum	nya
kau	kao	ko
m'hai	plaw	ma–hok–pu
an chau	(weyla) tiang	mun–te
pak	tit nüa	myauk
pey	chamük	na–kaung
m'	mai	ma
mo ye	mai mi arai	ba mya ma
yin choi	dio ni ; bat ni	ya–ku
so muk	lek ti	nam–bat
tim chung	mong ; nalika	na–yi
(ke)	k'ong	(i)
pan kong sat	ti tam ngan	yo–ne ; ofis
kun chöng	nai ta han	sit–bo
si söng	boi boi	a–kyeyn–jeyn
yau	nam–man	si
ho	tok-long	kaung–ba–byi
kau	kao	haung

ENGLISH	JAPANESE	CHINESE (M.)
on	–no ue ni	shang to
once	ichi do	i hui
one	ichi ; shto (–ts)	i (gaw)
only	dake ; tada	ji
open	aker–	kai chaw
or	ka	hwaw
orange	mikan	jü dzö
order, to	meyjir	van vu
other	ta	bieh
our	waga	waw men di
out	kara	chu
pack up	tsumer–	jwang
pain	itami	dang
paper	kami	ji
path	michi	shiau lu
pay, to	ur–	gey chieh
peace	anraku	tai ping
pen	pen	(i kwan) pi
pencil	empitsu	jien pi
people	jin	ren min
pepper	kosho	hu jiau mir
perfume	niwoi	shiang wey
person	shto ; nin ; jin	ren
picture	e	hwa ö
pig	buta	ju
pillow	makura	jan to
pin	hari	bang jan
pineapple	ananas'	bo lo mi
pipe	kiseru	yen dai
place	toko (–ro)	di vang

CHINESE (C.)	SIAMESE	BURMESE
choi	bon	a–paw–ma
yat si	ti nung	ta–li
yat	nung	ta
tuk	tao nan	tha
hey	pöt	pwin
wak che	rü	tho-ma-hok
chang	som	leym–maw
ming ling	sang	a–meyn–pey
pit	ün	acha
ngaw tey ke	k'ong rao	do
ngoi	nawk	a–pyin–ma
pau	gep-k'ong	tok
tung	puet	na–jin
chi	gradat	sa–yet–ywet
lo	tang dön	chi–lan
fu	chai	pey–sat–thi
waw peng	suk samran	yan–gun
mak söi pat	pakka	kalaung
yün pat	pinsaw	ke–dan
yan	k'on	thu–mya
wu chiu	pruk tai	nga–yok–kaung
hiong söi	nam hom	a–nan
yan	k'on	thu ; lu
söng ; wa	rup	jok–pon
chü	mu	wet
cham tau	mawn	gaung–on
cham	mut	twe–at
paw law	saparot	na–nat
yin tau	klong	sey-dan
tey fong	(satan) ti	a–ya

ENGLISH	JAPANESE	CHINESE (M.)
plain (ground)	maki–ba	su di
plant, a	kusa ; ueki	shu yang
plate	sara	pan dzö
play, to	hara– ; asob–	wan shwa
pocket	kakushi	do dzö
poisonous	doku na	du yau
policeman	junsi	shün bu
pond	ike	chö
pony	ma	ma
porter	ninsoku	gung ren
possess	mots–	yu
post office	yubin-kyoku	yü chang chü
pot	hachi	gwaw
potato	imo	shan yau
pour	tsug–	dau chu lai
prayer	inori	dau gau
present, to be	sanka sur–	shi ; dzai
price	ne (–dan)	jia chien
priest	senkyoshi	ji su
prince	kimi	chün wong
prisoner	horyo ; shunin	jien fan
profession	shokugyo	hwaw
pull	hik–	la
punish	tsumi sur–	ji dzui
purse	kane-ire	jien gia dzö
put	ok–	gaw shia
quarter	shibun no ichi	sö fan ji i
question	gimon ; mondai	i wan
quick	hayai	kwai

CHINESE (C.)	SIAMESE	BURMESE
peng tey	ti rap	kwin
sü	ton mai	a–pin
tip	chan	pa–gan–bya
wan sa	len	ka–za
toi	ka pao	eyk
tuk	pen pit	a–seyt
king chat	tam ruat	a–mu–dan
tawng	sa ; nong	in
ma tsai	ma krap	myin
kök fu	kon kon kong	kuli
yau	mi	shi
yau ching kuk	titamkan prais'ni	det–yon
po	maw	o
haw lan sü	man farang	a–lu
cham	tey	thun
key to	kam suat	su–daung–thi
tzoi	yu	pyit
ka chin	raka	a–po
waw söng	pra	sa–ya
tai tzi	momchan	min–tha
fan yan	nak tot	a–kyin–tha
chik yip	ngan achip	a–lok
lai	lak ; düng	swe–ngin
che tsi	long tot	a-pyit–dan
ho pau	ka pao ngön	tha–yey–eyk
fong	sai	ta
se fun yat	sio	ta–zeyt
man	kam tam	a–mey
fai	reo	lyin

ENGLISH	JAPANESE	CHINESE (M.)
rabbit	usagi	shan mau
rain	ame	yü
raisins	hoshi budo	pu to kan ö
rat	nezumi	hau dzö
railway	tetsudo	tieh dau
raw	nama	shang
razor	kami-sori	gwa lien dau
read, to	yom–; tokusho sur–	kan shu
ready	shitaku	hau law
receipt	uketori	sho chü
red	akai	hung
relation	shinrui	shüeh dzu
remember	oboer–	ji da
remove	ugokas–	naw
repair, to	naos-	shiu
reply, to	kotaer–	da bien
rescue, to	tas'ker–	jiu ji
rest (repose)	yasumu	shiu shi
return (go back)	kaer–	hui lai
rice (raw)	ine	dau dzö
rice (cooked)	han; meshi	mi van
rich	kanemochi	vu yu
ride, to	nor–	chi
rifle	shoju	lai vu jiang
right (side)	migi	yu sho
right (correct)	honto	dui law
ripe	jukush'ta	sho law
rise, to	agar–	chi lai
river	kawa	haw
road	michi	lu
roof	yane	vang ding

CHINESE (C.)	SIAMESE	BURMESE
to	katai	thimbaw–yon
yü	fon	mo yua jin
po tai tzi	luk angun hang	sa–byit–thi–jauk
lo sü	nu	chuet
tit lo	rot fai	mi–y'ta lun
sang	dip	seyn
tai to	mit kon	thin–don
tuk	an	pat
yü pey	set	pyin–zin
sau tan	bai rap	pyey–za
hung	si deng	ni
chun chik	yat	a-myo
ke tak	jam	mat–mi
yi tung	yai	yu–thwa
sau ching	ka	pyin–zin
wö i	tawp	tu–j'yey
kau	chuey	ke–tin
on sit	nawn pak	eyk–pyaw
fan höi	klap pai	pyan–thwa
mai	k'au san	san ; z'ba
fan	k'au suk	ta–min
yau chin	ruey	kyu–e–wa
ke	k'i	si
chöng	pün	yik–pat
yau sau	k'wa	let–ya–bet
ying koi	tuk	man
suk	suk	me
hey	(luk) k'ün	ta
haw	ma nam	myit
ło	tanon	lan
uk tang	lang k'a	a–mo

ENGLISH	JAPANESE	CHINESE (M.)
room	heya	wu dzö
rope	nawa	shang dzö
rotten	k'satta	vu bai law
rough	arai	ma ja
rug	ketto	jan dzö
run	hashir–	pau
sack	fukuro	ko dai
safe	daijobu	bau shien
salt	shio	bai yen
same	hito ; do	tung
sand	suna	sha dzö
sandals	waraji ; zori	tsau gwa da ö
sauce	kakeshiru ; shoyu	dziang
savage	mugoi ; yaban na	yeh
say	i– ; mos–	shwaw
scissors	hasami	jien dzö
school	gakko	shüeh shiau
screen	shoji	jang dzö
screw	neji	law sö ding
sea	umi	hai
seat	seki	dzo wey
second	dai ni	di ö
see	mir–	chiau
seek	sagas–	jau
sell	ur–	mai
send	okur– ; ya–	sung
seven	nana (–ts) ; shichi	chi (gaw)
several	oku no	ji gaw
sew	nu–	vang
shallow	asai	chien

CHINESE (C.)	SIAMESE	BURMESE
fong	hong	a–kan
sing sok	chüek	cho–ji
wai	nao	ma kaung
hai	kru kra	kyan
tey chin	from	kaw–zaw
pau	wing	pyey
toi	kasawp	kwey–eyt
tet kiu	prawt fai	lon–chon
yim	klua	sa
tung	müan gan	a tu tu
sa	sai ; trai	the
taw hai	rong taw ta	chi–nin
chöng	nam saws	sa–me
san fan	du	a–myet
kong (wa)	klao	pyaw
kau chin	tagrai	kat–chi
hok tong	rong rien	sa–thin–jaung
lim	lap la	ka–la–ga
law si	sikru	twe–at
hoi	tale	pin–le
cho wai	ma nang	ka–la–ting
tai i	ti song	du–ti–ya
kin	du	myin
cham	tio ha	sha
mai	k'ai	yaung
key	song	phot–thi
chat	lai	ku–nit
key yöng	yep	taw daw mya
lün	weyla	chok
chin	tün	tain thi

ENGLISH	JAPANESE	CHINESE (M.)
shave, to	sor–	gwa lien
shawl	kesa	bey vang
sheep	hitsuji	yang
she	ano onna	ta
sheet	uwa-shiki	bey dan ö
ship	fune	chwan
shirt	shatsu	han shan
shoe	kutsu	shieh
shoot, to	ir-	vang
shop	mise	pu dzö
short	mijikai	twan
shoulder	kata	jien bang ö
shout, to	donar–	ku
show, to	miser–	jau gan gan
side	kata ; ho	bien
sign	shirushi	dzö
sign, to	kimey sur–	ming
silk	kinu	sö
silver	gin	yin
since	irai	sung
sir	san	nin na
sister	ane	jieh jieh
sit	suwar–	dzaw
six	roku ; mu	liu gaw
skin	hifu	pi
skirt	suso	jün dzö
sky	ten ; sora	tien
sleep, to	ner–	shui
slow	osoi	man
small	chi'isai ; semai	shiau
smell, a	nioi	wan i wan

CHINESE (C.)	SIAMESE	BURMESE
tai	kon nuet	san yeyk
pey fung	pa pan kaw	ta–bet
yöng	ka	tho
küi	k'au	thu (–ma)
pey tan	papu ti non	a–chut
sün	rüa ; kampan	thim–baw
chan sam	süa chöt	kambiza
hai	rong tao	chi–nin
ta	ying	th'nat pyit
tim	hang	sing
tün	san ; tia	to
pawk tau	ba	pa–kon
ai	takon	kaw ; laik
yü	s'dang	pya
pin	kang	na–bey
key ho	krüang mai	yok–pon
chim	kian chü	let–mat to
si	mai	po
ngan	ngön	ngwey
key yin	tang ta	nauk
sin sang	kra pom	bo–ji ; kin–bya
chi mui	pi saw ; nong saw	a–ma
chaw	nang	ting
luk	hok	chauk
pey	nang	a–yey
kwan	sarong	lun–ji
tin	fa	mo kaung gin
süi	nawn	eyk–pyaw
man	cha	ney
siu	lek	nge ; they
mey	klin	a–nan

ENGLISH	JAPANESE	CHINESE (M.)
smoke	kemuri	yen
smoke, to	nom–	chi yen
snake	hebi	chang chung
snow	yoki	shüeh
so	so	(i yang) di
soap	shabon	i dzö
socks	kutsu-sh'ta	wa dzö
soft	yawarakai	jwan
soil	tochi	di
soldier	gunjin ; heysots'	bing ding
some	aru	shieh haw
something	nanzo	dung shi
sometimes	itsu ka	yo di shö ho
son	musuko	ö dzö
song	utau–mono	chang
soon	chikai uchi	kwai
sorry	kinodoku	gan
sort	shina	yang
soup	soppu	tang
sour	suppai	swan
south	minami	nan
speak	hanas–	shwaw
spectacles	megane	yen ching dzö
spend	tsuka	vey
spices	kosho	la'
spoon	saji	chi dzö
spring, a	izumi	jing
stable	maya	ma hau
stairs	hashigo	ti dzö
stamp (postal)	yubin–sey	yu biau
stand, to	tats–	jan ju

CHINESE (C.)	SIAMESE	BURMESE
yin	kwan fai	mi–go
sik yin	saup	thauk
se	ngu	mwey
süt	yesi hima	mo–bwin
kam yöng	dang nan	to–tho
kan	sabu	sat–pya
mat	tung tau san	chi–zut
yün	awn	pyaw
tey mai	din	myey
ping	ta–han	sit–tha
key	bang	t'cho
yau mat	kong bang yang	t'zon t'ku
yau si	bang ti	ta–ka
chai	but chai	tha
kaw	pleng	bun
chöng kan	reo–reo ni	my ma–kya
haw sik	ser–chai	seyt–pu jin
yong	kanat ; yang	a–myo
tong	kang chüt	a–pyok–yi
sün	priu	chin
nam	tit tai	taung
kong	put	so
ngan keng	wan ta	myet–man
sai chin	chai	pey–sat–thi
hiong liu	krüang tet	nga–yok–kaung
chi kang	chawn	zun
chün	′nam) pu	yey–san
ma fong	rong ma	nwa–tin–gok
lau tai	gra dai	ley–ga
yau piu	prais'ni yakawn	t'zaka kaung
key	yün	yat

ENGLISH	JAPANESE	CHINESE (M.)
star	hoshi	shing shing
starch	nori	dian
start, to	hajimer–	chi lai
station, police	keysatsusho	ging ja gü
station, railway	teyshaba	ho je jan
stay, to	nokor–	dzai
steal	uba– ; nusum–	to
steamer	jokisen	lwan jwan
steel	hagane	gang
stick	tsue	tang dzö
sting, a	hari	ku tung
stocking	nagakutsu–sh'ta	wa dzö
stomach	hara	du dzö
stone	ishi	shi to
stop, to	tomer–	jan ju ba
storm	arashi	bau vang
story	hanashi	shau hwa
straight	zutto	ji
stranger	tanin	kaw ren
street	tori	jieh
strike, to	buts–	da
string	ito	shang dzö
strong	kitsui ; jobu	yu jin ö
study, to	manab–	shüeh
sugar	sato	tang
summer	natsu	shia dien
sun	hi ; taiyo	tai yang
supper	yumeshi	wan van
swamp	numa	ni
swim	oyog–	vu shue

CHINESE (C.)	SIAMESE	BURMESE
sing	dao	che
chiong fan	pang	si
hey tau	awk chak ; röm	a-sa pyu
king chat kuk	rong pak ; satani	dana
ho chet chan	satani rot fai	bu da yon
hit	yut yu	ney
tau	k'a moi	ko
faw sün	rüa fai	mi thim–baw
kong	lek	than–mani
sü kan	mai	dọk
chi	lek nai tüa püng	kok
mat	tung tao yao	chi–zut–shey
to	tawng	baik
sak	hin	chauk
ting	yut	yat
tai fung	payu	mon–ding
ku	rüang	vi–thu
chik	trong	pyaung
ngoi hak yan	kon plak na	da byey tha
kai	tanon	eyn–dan–lan
ta	ti	kok
sin	chüek	cho–ji
köng	keng reng	sun–ma
hok	rien	thin
tong	nam tan	tha–ja
ha tin	na ron ; rüdu ron	nwey–u–du
tai yöng	pra atit ; dat	ney
man chan	ahan yen	nya–za
sap tey	nong ; büng	seyn-myey
yau süi	wai nam	yey ku

ENGLISH	JAPANESE	CHINESE (M.)
table	tsukue	jaw dzö
tailor	shitateya	tsai veng
take away	tor–	ba
take (hold of)	tor– ; nigir–	na
talk, to	henji sur–	shwaw
tank (reservoir)	midzutame	jö
tea	cha	cha
teach	oshier–	jiau
teacher	kyoju	giau shi
telegram	dempo	dien bau
tell, to	kikaser–	gau sö
temple	jinja ; tera	sö ; kwan
ten	ju ; to ; jippiki	shi (gaw)
tent	temmaku	jang bang
than	yeri	bi
that	are ; sore	na gaw
their	ano sh'to no	ta men di
then	sono toki	ho lai
there	sochi; soko ni	na li
therefore	sore des kara	so yi
they	ano sh'to	ta men
thick	atsui	ho
thief	dorobo	dzey
thin	hosoi	bau
thing	mono	shu ching; tung shi
think	omo–	shiang
this	kore	ja gaw
thousand	sen	chien
thread	ito	shien
three	san ; mi	san (gaw)
throw, to	nager–	jang

CHINESE (C.)	SIAMESE	BURMESE
toi	to	sa–bwe
choi fung	chang yep pa	a–chok–thama
law	rip ; aw pai	yu–thwa
cha	chap ; song	yu
kong	kui	pyaw ; so
chi	kra pang ; tang	yey–gan
cha	nam cha	la–pet–yi ; l'pey
kau	sawn	thin–cha
sin sang	kru	saya
tin po	(kam) tor'leyk	kyey–nan
kong	bok	pyaw
miu	wat	zey–di
sap	sip	ta se
chöng mok	k'ai	tai
pey	kwa	det
kawkaw	nan	to ; ho
köi ke	k'ong k'au	thu–do
kaw si	leo	to a–ka–nik
kaw to	ti nun	ho–ma
so yi	fro chanan	to–jaung
köi tey	k'au	thu–do
hau	na	pyit ; tok
chak	ka moi	tha–ko
pok	bang	pa
kin si ; mat kin	kong ; tu ra	a–ya
siong	kit	tin
ni ko	ni	thi
yat chin	pan	taung
sin	dai	chi
sam	sam	thon
pek	ting ; yon	pit

ENGLISH	JAPANESE	CHINESE (M.)
ticket	kippu	biau dzö
tie, to	shibar–	jieh
time	toki ; tabi	shi ho ö
tin	suzu	ma ko tieh
to	–ni	(key)
today	kyo	jin tien
together	kanete	dung
tomorrow	myonichi ; ash'ta	ming tien
tonight	komban	gin wan
too (much)	amari ; yokey	ding
tooth	ha	ya
torch	tai–matsu	(i jan) dang
touch, to	sawar–	ti
towards	ye	shang
towel	tonogui	sho gin
tower	yagura	ta
town	tokai	chang
track	michi	lu
trade, to	akina–	shang yeh
train (railway)	kisha	o je
translate, to	honyaku sur–	tung i
travel, to	ryoko sur–	lü shing
traveller	tabi–bito	yu li geh
tree	ki	shu
tribe	shuzoku	cha
trousers	zubon	ku dzö
true	shin	jan
try, to	mir–	shi i shi
turban	hachimaki	dau gan
twelve	ju ni (–tto)	shi ö (gaw)
twenty	ni ju	ö shi (gaw)

CHINESE (C.)	SIAMESE	BURMESE
piu	tua	let–mat
pong kan	fuk	lon–chon
si	weyla	ka–la
sek	dibuk	than–byu
(to)	su ; ti	ko ; tho ; a
kum yat	wan ni	ya–ney
yat chai	pa kan	nin–a–tu
ting yat	prung ni	ma–net–pyan
kam man	kün ni	ya–ku–nya
tai	gönpai	lun
nga	fan	thwa
faw pa	fai–chai ; tai	let-neyk dam–mi
mo	ta	ti to
hiong	pai su	tho
min kan	pa k'on	let–thok–pa–wa
tap	haw	dok
seng	müang ; chiang	myo
lo	tang (pa)	lan
tso sang yi	k'a k'ai	yaung
faw che	rot fai	ya–ta
fan-yik	pla	pyan zo
löi hang	tong tio ; dön tang	ka–yi–thwa
löi hak	nak tong tio	da byey tha
sü	ton mai	chon
chuk	chat	pyi–thu pyi–tha
fu	kang keng	baumbi
chan	ching	man
si	long	san
tau kan	muak kek	gaung–baung
sap yi	sip–song	se na
yi sap	yi–sip	na se

ENGLISH	JAPANESE	CHINESE (M.)
twice	nido	liang bien
two	ni ; fta (–ts) ; fu	liang ; ö
umbrella	kasa	san
under	–no shita ni	shia
understand	waka–	shau dö
uniform	gumpuku	hau i
up	uye ni	shang bien
us	watashi domo	waw men
useful	choho	yu yung
valley	tani	shan gu
value	atai	gwey jung di
vegetables	yasai	dzai su
veil	kinu–katsugi	lien dzö
very	yohodo ; taiso	han ; ding
village	sato ; mura	tsun jwang ö
visit, to	homon sur–	bai
wages	kyukin	gung chien
wait, to	mats–	dang
wake, to	me ga samer–	shing law
walk, to	aruk–	dzo
wall	kabe	chiang
want, to	nozom–	yau
war	ikusa ; senso	jan jang
warm	attakai	nwan haw
was	deshta	la
wash, to	ara–	shi
washerman	sentaku–ya	shi i–shang ti
watch (clock)	tokey	biau

CHINESE (C.)	SIAMESE	BURMESE
liong bai	song ti	na
liong ; yi	song	na
che	rom	ti–let
ha tai	tai	auk-ma
ming	k'ao chai	na–le
chai fuk	krüang bab	sin du
söng ko	k'ün	a–paw–tho
ngaw	tey rao	do–go
yau yung	pen prayot	a–thon–win
san kak	hup k'au	ching
ga chin	k'a	a–po
choi	pak	hin–yuet
lim	pa klum na	myet–na–pon
kek chi	mak	te
hiong chün	(mu) ban ; tambon	ywa
tam	pai yiam	twei
kung chin	ngön duan	nwe
tang	raw	ney
ching seng	pluk	no
lo hang	dön	thwa
chiong	kampang	ta–ding
oi	tong kan	chin
ching	song–kram	sit
nün	un	nwey ; ik
hai	dai (pen)	–de ; –pyi
sai	sak ; lang	sey
sai yi yan	k'on sak pa	ka–wa–the
piu	na-lika	na–yi–gwet

English	Japanese	Chinese (M.)
watch, to	mamor–	gwan
watchman	bampey	gan man di
water	mizu	shue
water, drinking	nomi–mizu	hö di shue
way	tori	dau ; lu
we	watashi–domo	waw men
weak	yowai	me yö chin
weapon	bu–ki	jün giai
week	shukan	i li bai
were	deshta	la
west	nishi	shi
wet	shimeppoi	shi law
what ?	dore ; nani	shan maw
wheel	kuruma ; wa	lun dzö
when ?	itsu	daw dzan
where ?	dochi	na li
which ?	dono ; dore	na gaw
white	shiroi	bai
who ?	dare	shui
why ?	naze	haw gu
wide	hiroi	kwan
wife	nyobo ; okusan	vu ren
will (shall)	–u desho	yau
wind (air)	kaze	vang
window	mado	chwang hu
wine	budo–shu	jiu
winter	fuyu	dung tien
wire	tesen	die sö
with	–de ;–to	gen ; na
without	naku	wu
woman	onna	nü ren

CHINESE (C.)	SIAMESE	BURMESE
chöng	hen ; du	zaung
hon sau yan	k'on yam	ta ga zaung
söi	nam ; tuk	yey
yan ke söi	nam kin	thauk–yey
lo	tang	lan
ngaw tey	rau	ch'nok do
yök	awn a	a–ne
ley hey	awut	len–net
lai pai	atit ; sa pa da	a–bat
hai	dai (pen)	–de ; –pyi
sai	tit t'wan tok	a–nauk
sap	piek	so
mat ye	arai	ba
lön	law	sat–they
ke si	mürai	be daw le
pin chu	ti nai	be le
pin yöng	an nai	be thin
pak	si kao	pyu
pin kaw	k'rai	be thu
tim kai	tam mai	ba jaung le
fat	kwang	kye
fu yan	panyara	ma–ya
oi	cha	me
fung	lom	ley–tik–chin
chöng mun	na tang	pa–din–bauk
tsau	lao angun	sa–byit–yi
tung tin	na nao ; rüdu nao	saung–u–du
tung sin	luet	cho–ji
kung	duey	nin
mo	mai mi	ma–shi–be
nui yan	pu ying	meyn–ma

ENGLISH	JAPANESE	CHINESE (M.)
wood	ki	mu to
word	kotoba	dzö
work (noun)	gyo ; hataraki	hwaw ; gung
workman	shokunin	gung ren
worse	motto warui	gang bu hau
worship	rey–hai	bai
wound, a	kega	shang ko
wrap up	tsutsum–	bau chi lai
write	kak(er)–	shieh
wrong	warui	tsaw law
year	nen ; toshi	nien
yellow	ki–iroi	hwang
yes	hey	shi di
yesterday	kino ; sakujitsu	dzaw tien
you	anata	ni
young	wakai	nien ching
your	anata no	ni ti

CHINESE (C.)	SIAMESE	BURMESE
muk	mai	dok
wa	kam	sa
kung fu	ngan	a–lok
si fu	k'on tam ngan	tha ma
kan wai	leo kwa	tha yuey so
pai	bucha	su–daung
söng	pla	a–na a-sa
pau	pan	tok
se	kien	yey–tha
m'chok	pit	ma man; ma–lwe
nin	pi	nit
wong	si lüang	wa
hai	krap	ho'ba
tsawk yat	müa wan ni	ma–ney
ney	tan ; k'un	kin–bya
nün	num ; dek	a–thet nge
ney ke	k'ong tan	maung–min

JAPANESE

Notes :

WORD ORDER : ' The ' and ' a, an ' are omitted. Prepositions (properly called postpositions) follow the words to which they refer. Adjectives precede nouns. Pronouns are often omitted. The verb always comes at the end of each sentence.

VERBS : Add the following endings to the roots given in the word-list to show tense, etc :—

Root–*imas'* . .	present (e.g. ' I am going ')
Root–*imasen* .	negative (' I am not going ')
Root–*imasho* .	future (' I will go ')
Root–*imasumai* .	negative future (' I won't go ')
Root–*imash'ta* .	past (' I went')
Root–*imasen-deshta*	negative past (' I didn't go')
Root–*inasai*. .	command (' Go ! ')
Root–*anaide–i–i* .	negative command (' don't go ! ')
o–Root–*ikudasai* .	request (' please go ')
o–Root–*ikudasaimas'na*	negative request (' please don't go ')

Verbs do not change to indicate different persons ;

thus, 'he goes' can only be distinguished from 'they go' by the context.

PLURALS: Nouns and adjectives do not change to indicate the plural.

NUMERATIVE PARTICLES: When a number is used with a noun, a numerative particle (similar to the word 'piece' in the Pidgin English phrase 'one piece house') must be used. The commonest particles are:

ka or *ko* .	for almost any noun
hai . .	for cupfuls, glassfuls, etc.
hiki . .	for animals, fish, etc.
ken . .	for buildings
mey or *nin*	for people
tsu . .	for documents

The order is: noun, number, particle. Thus, 'one soldier' becomes 'soldier one person' (*heyshi ichi-mey*).

OTHER PARTICLES: These play an important part in the make-up of colloquial Japanese. The commonest are:

ga .	indicates the nominative case.
ka .	indicates a question.
no .	generally links a noun to an adjective or a verb.
wa .	emphasizes the word it follows.
wo .	indicates the accusative case.
ya .	normally suggests doubt.

These particles follow the words to which they refer.

JAPANESE

Special List :

ancestor	senzo
bamboo	take
bean curd	tofu
be careful !	ki wo tsukero
bicycle	jitensha
boatman	sendo
bowl	wan
box, lacquered	jubako
brush, writing	fude
Buddha, a	hotoke
Buddhism	bukkyo
Buddhist priest	bosan
camera	shashinki
China	shina ; kara
cherry tree	sakura
chopsticks	hashi
coat, Japanese	haori
coolie	ninsoku
crab	kani
Christianity	yasokyo
don't mention it	do itashimash'te
England	eykoku ; igirisu
emperor	kotey
European clothes	yof'ku
excuse me !	moshi; gomen kudasai

famous place	meysho
fireworks	hanabi
flea	nomi
fried food	suwaki
Formosa	taiwan
Germany	doitsu
go away!	achi ike
god (Shinto)	kami
godown, warehouse	kura
goodbye	sayonara
good morning	o hayo
good night	oyasumi nasai
grapes	budo
I don't know	shira
it is (2) o'clock	(ni)–ji
Japan	nihon; nipon
Japan, made in	wasey
Japanese Empire	teykoku
Jesus	yaso
Korea	chosen
local speciality	meybutsu
Manchuria	manshu (koku)
melon	uri
millet	awa
Occident, the West	seyo; o-bey
official	shikwan; kwannin

onion	negi
pagoda	to
palace	yash'ki
parasol	kasa
peach	momo
pear	nashi
persimmon . . .	kaki
photograph(–er) . .	shashin (–ki)
please, if you . . .	doka ; dozo
rice-field . . .	ta
rickshaw	kuruma
rickshaw-puller . .	kurumaya ; shafu
rumour	hyoban
Russia	ro–koku ; rosha
scroll (hanging) . .	kakemono
shrine	miya
singing-girl . . .	geysha
soya	shoyu
squat, to . . .	suwar–
suicide	jisatsu ; harakiri
sweetmeat made of beans and sugar	yokan
sweet potato . . .	satsuma–imo
sword . . .	katana
temple (Shinto) . .	jinja ; yashiro
,, (Buddhist) . .	tera
thank you . . .	arigato
that won't do . .	ikenai

U.S.A.	beykoku ; gashukoku
veranda	engawa
volcano	kwazan
warrior	samurai
wrestling . . .	sumo ; judo ; jujitsu
what's the matter ? . .	nanda
what's the time ? . .	mo nanji des

Names of Countries : Add *-go* or *-kotoba* to these to form the name of the corresponding language ; add *-jin* to indicate a man of the country concerned ; add *-no* to form the simple adjective applying to that country.

CHINESE

Notes :

PRONUNCIATION : The Chinese languages are tonal ; that is to say, the meaning of a word varies according to the tone in which it is uttered. The only way to master the correct tones for Chinese words is to listen to a Chinese speaker.

There is no clear distinction in the Chinese languages between hard and soft consonants (e.g., k and g, p and b). Thus, g sounds like something between the English g and k, and so on.

In Cantonese a final k, p or t is cut short, and it is barely possible to distinguish a final k from a final p or t.

ORDER : The Chinese prefer short, terse sentences, and omit all superfluous words. In simple phrases the order is generally the same as in English. ' The ' and ' a ' are omitted.

PLURALS, ETC. : Chinese nouns, adjectives and verbs do not change ; there are no endings or prefixes such as in other languages denote gender, case, tense, mood, number, etc.

PREPOSITIONS : Some precede the noun, some follow. Where in the word-lists a preposition is followed by a dash, it precedes the noun ; where it is shown preceded by a dash, it follows the noun. ' Of ' is translated as if it were English ' 's ' ; the order in Chinese is therefore not 'top : of : mountain' but 'mountain : of ('s) : top.'

Verbs : Tense is sometimes indicated simply by the context, sometimes by a word placed before or after the verb, just as in English we use 'will', 'did,' etc.

yau before the verb indicates the future ('will')
tsang before, or *la* after, the verb indicates the past ('did', 'was', etc.)
pey before the verb indicates the passive.
ba after the verb indicates a command.

Questions : In a question the word order remains the same as in a plain statement, but the sentence must end with an interrogative word such as 'how', 'who', or 'when', or with one of the interrogative particles *ma*, *maw* and *ni*; these correspond roughly to the English particle 'eh ?' at the end of a question.

Numerative Particles : When a noun follows a number (including the number 'one'), a numerative particle (corresponding to the word 'piece' in the Pidgin English phrase 'One piece house') must be placed between number and noun. The commonest particles are :

	(Mandarin)	(Cantonese)	
for almost any noun .	*gaw* .	*chak*	(piece)
for animals . . .	*to* .	*taw*	(head)
for clothing, houses, etc.	*jien* .	*tso*	(part)

Thus 'one man' becomes 'one piece man', i.e. : *i gaw ren* (Mandarin) : *yat chak yan* (Cantonese).

CHINESE

Special List :

	MANDARIN	CANTONESE
amber	hu paw	fu pak
America	ya–mey–li–ka	ya–mey–li–ka
apricot	shing dzö	moi
bamboo	ju dzö	chuk
banana	shiang chau	kung tsiu
be careful !	do gai	siu sam
camel	law taw	lok to
China	jung gwaw	chung kwok
chopsticks	kwai dzö	fai tzi
crab	pang shieh	hai
crackers (squibs)	bien	pau chöng
Christian	ji du	chi tu ; ye-su chau-yan
dragon	(i diau) lung	lung
England	ying gwaw	ying kwok
Europe	o–lo–pa	ngau chau
excuse me	dwey bu ju	toi pat chu
fig	wu hwa go	mo fa kwaw
fireworks	bien	yin faw
Formosa	tai wan	toi wan
France	va gwaw	fat kwok

fruits :		
(akin to grapes)	li–chi	lai chi
(small orange)	kin kü	kam kwot
(peach-like)	pi–pa	lu kwot
(lemon)	shiang tau	ning mung
(lime)	bai hui	fui
(melon)	shiang gwa	hiong kwa
(peach)	dau dzö	to
(pear)	li	ley
(plum)	li dzö	moi
(quince)	mu gwa	muk kwa
Germany	de gwaw	tak kwok
ghost	maw gwey	kwai
go away !	ni jü ba	chau hoi
good-bye	dzai chen	choi wöi
good morning	ni hau mo	ni ho ma
have you eaten your rice ? (usual greeting)	ni chi la fan mey yu ?	ni sik yün fan mey a ?
I don't know	wo bu dzi u dau	ngaw m'tzi to
India	yin du	yen to
it is 2 o'clock	ö tien jung	löng tim chung
ivory	shiang ya	chiong nga
Japan	ri ban gwaw	yet pun kwok
lantern	dang lung	tang lung
mah jong	ma jong	ma chök

mandarin, official	gwan	kun fu
monsoon	fu dien	fuk tien
never mind	bu ai sirr	mo man tai
nut	haw ö	hat tze
opium	ya pien yen	a pen
pagoda	ta	tap
please, if you	jing bien	ching ne
prawns	ma	ha
Russia	o gwaw	ngaw kwok
satin	cho dzö	tün
teapot	cha hu	cha u
temple	miau	kwan
thank you	shieh shieh ni	taw tze
veranda	chwan lang	tin toi
what is the time ?	ji tien jung	ke tim chung
what's the matter?	shan mo sirr	cho m'si

Military words (Mandarin only):

general . . . . shang giang
colonel . . . . shang siau
major . . . . shau siau
captain . . . . shang we
lieutenant . . . rung we
sergeant . . . . rung shi

private	bing ding
company	lien
battalion	ying
brigade	lu

Names of Countries : By dropping *gwaw* and *kwok* and adding *hwa* (Mandarin) and *wa* (Cantonese), these become the names of the corresponding languages ; and by substituting *ren* (Mandarin) and *yan* (Cantonese), they come to denote a man of the country concerned. Thus, in Cantonese, *ying kwok* is England, *ying wa* English, and *ying yan* Englishman.

SIAMESE

Notes :

PRONUNCIATION : Like Chinese, Siamese is tonal ; there are five different tones, and the meaning of a word varies according to the tone in which it is pronounced. The only way to learn how to pronounce a Siamese word in the correct tone is to listen to a Siamese saying it.

WORD ORDER : 'The' and 'a, an' are omitted. In general, word order is the same as in a simple English sentence.

PREPOSITIONS : These are often omitted ; when used, they usually precede the noun.

VERBS : Each verb has only one form ; there are no endings or prefixes. Tense, mood and person are shown either by context (e.g. 'I go yesterday' ; 'I go next week') or by the presence of *cha* ('will') and *dai* ('was') and the personal pronouns *chan* ('I'), tan ('you'), *kau* ('he' or 'she'), *mau* ('it'), *rau* ('we') and *kau* ('they').

The verb 'to be' is generally omitted.

PLURALS : There is no change for the plural in nouns, adjectives or verbs.

QUESTIONS : Interrogative words such as 'where ?', 'who ?' and 'how ?' are placed at the end of a sentence.

NUMERATIVE PARTICLES: When a noun is linked to a number (including 'one') a particle is placed after number and noun on the model of the Pidgin English phrases 'one piece shoe', 'three piece fish', etc. The commonest particles are:

an . .	for any class of noun
bai . .	for flat things (dishes, pages, sheets)
haw .	for packets, parcels, etc.
k'on .	for people
luk . .	for round things (e.g. fruit)
lang .	for buildings
ton . .	for trees and plants
tua . .	for animals, clothes, furniture, and wooden or iron things such as tools.

The order in a phrase of this kind is: noun, number, particle. Thus 'five soldiers' becomes 'soldier five piece' (*tahan ha k'on*).

SIAMESE

Special List:

Annamite, -ese . .	yuan
Ayuthia . . .	krungkao
bamboo . . .	mai pai; pa pai
banana . . .	kluai
Bangkok . . .	krungtep
battalion . . .	kong pan
battle . . .	kang rop
betel-nut (palm) . .	mak; (ton mak)

boat, flat-bottomed .	kuhle
bring that here . .	au nan ma ni
Buddhism . . .	putasasana
buffalo . . .	kwai ; wua
Burma, Burmese . .	pama
bush country . .	pa hya
captain . . .	nai roi ek
Cambodian . .	kamrat müang kamen
cart-track . . .	tang kwian
Ceylon . . .	ko langka
Chinese . . .	chek ; chin
Chinese temple . .	san chau
Chinese theatre . .	ngiu
cholera . . .	ahiwa takarok
clan	puak
clearing in jungle . .	tang pa ; pa la mo
cocoanut . . .	(pon) maprao
cocoanut palm . .	ton maprao
crab	pu
crocodile . . .	choroke
custard apple . .	noi na
colonel . . .	nai pan ek ; nai pan to
corporal (mily.) . .	nai sip to
company (mily.) . .	kong roi
Danish . . .	hang pratet denmak
Denmark . . .	denmak
division (mily.) . .	kiak kai ; kong pon to
do you understand ? .	kau chai rü
dry season . . .	rüdu leng
durian . . .	turien

elephant . . .	chang
elephant-driver . .	kwan chang
English . . .	angkrit
European . . .	farang
ferry	rüa cheo ; ta rüa chang
fire-crackers . .	pratat
foot (approximately 12″)	küp
French . . .	farangsat
general (mily.) . .	nai pon ek
German . . .	yerman
good-bye . . .	la (pai kon)
government office . .	sala rataban
government department	krom
harbour . . .	ta rüa
headman . . .	pu hyai ban ; chao müang
howdah . . .	kup
how do you do ? . .	tan sa-bai di rü
image . . .	rup kao rop
Indian . . .	kek
Indian temple . .	wat kek
is it true ? . . .	ching rü
it is true . . .	ching pen na
Japan . . .	yipun
jungle fever . .	kai pa
jungle, dense . .	dong tüp
jungle mixed with cultivated land . .	pon pa

junk (Chinese ship)	tapao
Karen	krieng
kerosene	namman kat
landing-place	ta nam
lizard	chin chok
lotus	dok bua
magistrate (rural)	kamnan
major (mily.)	nai pan tri
malaria	kai püa yung
Malay	malayu
mango	mamnang
mangrove	pa lampu
mile (approximately)	si sip sen ; mail
monastery	aram
monks (Buddhist)	pra
monsoon	lam ta pao
monsoon season	rüdu lom
mosquito	yung
mosquito net	mung
never mind	mai pen-rai
opium	ya fin
paddy-field	tung na
palace	wang ; prasat
palm tree	ton tan ; ton lan
Penang	ko hmak
picul (133 lbs.)	hap

plantation . . .	rai suan
priest's cell . . .	kuti
private (mily.) . .	pon ta–han
quinine . . .	ya kao ke kai
regiment . . .	kong krom
rest-house . . .	sala ; rong asai
rhinoceros . . .	ret
rickshaw . . .	rot chek
rice-fields, countryside .	na
scorpion . . .	malang pong
sergeant . . .	nai sip ek
shark	pla chlam
Siam	sayam
Siamese . . .	t'ai
sweet potato . .	man teyt
sword . . .	dap
take care ! . . .	rawang
tamarind . . .	makam
teak	mai sak
theatre . . .	la–kon
ticul (formerly 2s.) .	bat
tiger	süa
veranda . . .	rabiang
very well . . .	sabai cha
warehouse . . .	kotakan
waterfall . . .	nam tok
water-lily . . .	bua

BURMESE

Notes :

PRONUNCIATION : Final k or t is cut very short. There is no clear distinction between hard and soft consonants (e.g. k and g, t and d). Like Chinese and Siamese, Burmese is a tonal language ; a single word may have three different meanings, distinguishable only by the tone in which it is uttered. These tones can only be learnt by listening to a Burmese speaker.

WORD ORDER : Verbs are placed at the end of sentences. Adjectives either follow nouns, or are placed before nouns with the syllable *–thaw–* between adjective and noun. Prepositions (more properly called postpositions) follow nouns. ' The ' and ' a ' are omitted. Pronouns and other words are often omitted when they are not required to make the meaning of a sentence clear ; e.g. ' I do not know ' becomes simply ' not know '. Word order does not change in asking questions ; the question is shown by placing the syllable *–la* after the verb.

PLURALS : The plural of nouns is usually shown by adding *–mya* (for inanimate things) or *–do* (for people and animals).

VERBS : The following syllables are added to verbs to show tense :

–thi or *–de* .	. present
–pyi or *–de* .	. past
–mi or *–me* .	. future
–ba . .	. command

Negative forms :

m' – Verb *–bù*	. ordinary negative
m' – Verb *–ne*	. negative command

Passive form :

a – Verb *–kan*

Verbs do not change to indicate plural or gender.

NUMERATIVE PARTICLES : When a noun follows a number (including the number 'one'), a particle (corresponding to 'piece' in the Pidgin English phrase 'one piece house') must be used. The order is : noun, number, particle. The commonest particles are :

yauk for people : thus, *lu ta yauk :* man one (person)

kaung for animals : thus, *nwa ta kaung :* ox one (animal)

ku for other things : thus, *le ta ku :* cart one (thing)

BURMESE

Special List :

Akyab . . .	sit-twey
America . . .	ameyika
anna . . .	t'be
Arakanese . .	ya-king

banana	n'pyaw–thi
Bassein	p'theyn
be careful !	thadi pyu-ba
be silent !	teyt–teyt
Buddhist	bok–da–yan
Burma	ba–ma
cholera	wan–yaw–ga
China	ta–yok–pyi
Christian	ka–yit–yan
coconut	on-thi
crab	ga-nan
creek	chaung
curry	hin
custard-apple	aw–za
deer (barking–)	ji
dragon	na–ga
durian	du–yin
dysentery	thwey–wan–na
elder (in a village)	lu–ji
elephant	sin
England	inga–leyk
Europe	u–yaw–pa
go away !	thwa–lik
gong	maung
good-bye	thwa–on–daw ; thwa–daw me-naw
headman	th'ji
how do you do ?	ma–ba–i–la

I am well . .	ma–ba–i
I don't know . .	ma thi–bu
India . . .	eyndia ; k'la
it is (2) o'clock . .	(na) na–yi
Japan . . .	za–pan
landing-place . .	thim–baw–zeyk
lemon . . .	shauk–chin
lizard . . .	eyn myaung ; tauk–te
malaria . . .	net-pya
Malay . . .	pa-shu
mango . . .	tha–yet–thi
Martaban . .	mot–ta–ma
Mergui . . .	beyt
mongoose . .	mwey–ba
monk . . .	pon–ji
monastery . .	pon–ji chaung
monsoon . . .	mo–u–du
never mind ! . .	a–twet ma shi–ba–bu
pagoda . . .	pey–ya
papaya . . .	thimbaw–thi
parrot . . .	chet–tu–yuey
peacock . . .	daung–bo
petroleum . .	yey–nan ; das–si
pigeon . . .	ko
Prome . . .	pyi
Ramree . . .	yan–byey

Rangoon . . . yan–gon
ricefield . . . le
robe . . . thin-gan
rupee . . . t'jat
Siamese . . . yo-da-ya
spirit, ghost . . nat

Tavoy . . . twe
teak . . . chun
thank you (rarely used) kyey–zu tin–ba–thi
tide . . . di
tiger . . . ja

veranda . . . ka lauk swe
villager . . . ywa–tha
well done ! . . kaung bey
what's the matter ? . ba pyit–tha–le
what's the time ? . be–na na–yi she d'la

yam . . . myauk–yaung

Names of Countries : By adding *-lu-myo*, these become the corresponding adjectives. Thus : *ingaleyk-lu-myo*, English.

Part Three

MALAY

TAMIL

BENGALI

RUSSIAN

ENGLISH	MALAY	TAMIL
above	di'atas	meyl
absent	tid'ada	illadha
accident	chilaika	abath'thu
address	alamat	meyl vilasham
after	l'pas	–pin
afternoon	p'tang	maley
again	lagi s'kali	thirumba
age	umor	ayu
alive	hidop	uyirulla
all	samoa	shagala
all right	baila	nalla
allow	kasi terbulan	idang kodu–
alone	sorang sahaja	thaniyey
also	juga	–um
always	s'lalu	yeporludhum
and	dan ; pun	–um
angry	marah	kobam–ulla
animal	binatang	mirugam
ant	smut	yerumbu
anything	apa–apa	yad'onnu
are	ada	–
arm	tangan	kai
army	tentra	padey
around	kliling	–shurla
arrangement	aturan	udanpadu
arrive	sampai	sher–
ask	tanya ; minta	kel–
at	di	–il
back (noun)	blakang	mudhugu
bad	kurang bai'	ketta

BENGALI	RUSSIAN
opor	nad ; naverkhu
onupost'it	atsutstvyushchi
bipod	nyeachastni sluchai
t'ikana	adres
pore	posle
bikal	polden
abar	snova
bo'esh	starost
jibonto	zhivoi
shob	vsye
ach'a	khar'sho
korte deo–	rasreshit
ekla	odin ; odno
aro	takzhe ; tozhe
shorbodar	vsyeghda
ar	i
birokto	razserzheni
janoar	zhivotnoye
pipre	muravey
kich'ui	shto–nibut
—	—
hat'	ruka
polton	armiya
charidike	vokrug
bondobosto	ustroistvo
po'unchan–	priyekhat
jigesh kor– ; chao	sprosit
–e	u
pit	zad
k'rap ; mondo	plokho

ENGLISH	MALAY	TAMIL
bag	pundipundi	shakku
bandage	kain	kattu
barber	tukang chuko	pariyari
basket	bakul	kudey
bath (tub)	mandi	snanam
bathe	mandi	kuli–
bathroom	bilek mandi	snana arey
be	(ada)	—
beans	kachang	ulundhu
beautiful	chantek	alagiya
because	s'bab	padiyal
become	m'njadi	agu–
bed	t'mpat tidor	kattil ; padukey
bedroom	bilek tidor	padukey–y'arey
before (time)	dulu	–mun
begin	mula'i	thuvakku
behind	di blakang	pinney
bell	locheng	mani
below	dibawa	–in kirl
bench	bangku	vangu
best	yang bai'	uththanam
between	antara	–udey
big	b'sar	peria
bill (account)	surat hutang	bil
bird	burong	parawey
black	hitam	vishukoth'u
blacksmith	tukang b'si	kollan
blanket	selimut	kambal
blood	dara'	iratham
blue	biru	nilam
board	papan	palagey

BENGALI	RUSSIAN
t'oli	chemodan
kapor	bandazh
napit	parikmakhair
tukri	korzinka
gusl	vanna
chan kor–	kupatsya
gusl k'ana	vannaya komnata
—	—
shim	fasol
shundor	krasivo
karon	patamu shto
ho'o–	stanovitsya
charpai	krovat
shobar–g'ar	spalnaya
–purbe	da
shuru kor–	nachinat
pech'ane	s'zadi
g'anta	zvonok
nichu	pod
choki	skamya
shob che'e b'alo	luchshi
majk'ane	sredi
boro	balshoi
hishab	s'chyot
pak'i	ptitsa
kalo	chawni
lohar–mistri	kuznets
kombol	odeyalo
rokto	krov
nil	galuboi ; sini
tokta	doska

ENGLISH	MALAY	TAMIL
boat	sampan ; pra'u	padagu
boil, to	r'bus	kodhi–
bone	tulang	yelumbu
book	kitab ; buku	pustakam
boot	s'patu	nedun-chapathu
born, to be	beranak	pira–
box	p'ti	petti
boy	buda'	shinavan
brass	t'mbaga kuning	pithaley
bread	roti	rotti
break, to	bikin pechal	iru–
bribe, a	suap	kai–kuli
brick	batu–bata	shengal
bridge	j'mbatan	palam
brother	saudara	shagodharan
brush, a	sikat	burus
build	buat	kattu–
building	ruma	vidu
bullock	l'mbu	yerudhu
burn, to	bakar	yeri–
bush	pokok	chinne cheri
business	kerja	aluval
buy	bli	vangu–
by	oleh	–al
call (for)	pang-gil	arley–
camp	kampong	ur
can (is able)	boleh	–(k)akudum
cannot	ta'boleh	–(k)akudadhu
candle	dian	merlugu vathi
cane	rotan	kai kol

BENGALI	RUSSIAN
noka ; dingi	lodka
shid'o kor–	kipyet
har	kost
kitab ; boi	kniga
juta	batinok
janm–	radit
baksho	karobka
ch'ele	malchik
pitol	latun
ruti	khleb
b'anga–	slomat
g'ush	dar
int	kirpich
pul	most
b'ai	brat
burush	sh'chyotka
toeri kor–	stro'it
kuti	zdaniye
bolud	bik
poran–	zhech
gach	kustarnik
bebsha	dyelo
kin–	kupit
die	po ; s'
dak–	zvat
tambu	lager
par–	mozhet
par– na	nye mozhet
mombati	svyecha
chori	palka

ENGLISH	MALAY	TAMIL
carpenter	tukang kayu	tachan
carpet	permadani	shamukalam
carriage	kreta	karattey
cart	chikar	karattey
cat	kuching	puney
catch, to	tangkap	pidi–
cave	lobang	arey
ceiling	atap	areymeyt kattu
chain	rantai	shangili
chair	kursi	natkali
change, to	uba	mattu–
check (bill)	surat hutang	bil
chief	k'pala	nayagan
child	anak	shinavan
choose	piley	therindhedu–
church	greja	haleyam
cigarette	kretek	sigret
city	negri	nagaram
clean	bersi	shuttamana
clerk	krani	kumastha
climb	panjat	yeyru–
clock	jam	kadiyaram
cloth	kain	adey
clothes	pakaian	adey
cloud	awan	meygam
coat	baju	shattey
cock	ayam jantan	sheyval
coffee	kopi	kappi
cold	dingin ; s'juk	kulirchiyana
collar	krag	kallar
comb	sisir	shippu

BENGALI	RUSSIAN
ch'utor	plotnik
dari	kovyor
gari	vagon
gari	telyezhka
beral	koshka
gan–	poimat
gob'or	pogreb
ch'at	patalok
shekor	tsep
cher	stul
bodol kor–	peremenit
hishab	s'chyot
shordar	nachalnik
bach'a	rebyonok ; ditya
poch'ondo kor–	vibirat
girja	tserkof
sigret	papirosa
shohor	gorod
saf	chisti
babu	sluzhishchi
ut'–	vlezat
g'ori	ch'si
kapor	sukno
kapor chupor	adyezhda
meg'	tucha ; obl'ko
kot	syurtuk
morog	pyetukh
kafi	kofe
t'anda	khalodni
kalar	vaŕatnik
chiruni	greben

ENGLISH	MALAY	TAMIL
come	datang ; mari !	va–
concerning	deri hal	–peyril
cook, a	kuki	kokki
cook, to	masa	adu-
corner	tanjang	muley
correct	b'tul	niyayamana
cost (noun)	harga	viley
cotton	kapas	panju
count	hitong	yennu–
country	negri ; b'nua	nadu
courtyard	k'bun	mutham
cover, to	tutop	mudu–
cow	l'mbu b'tina	maru
crowd	kumpolan	kuttam
cup	mangkok	koppey
cupboard	lamari	kappordu
curtain	tirai	thirey
cushion	bantal	methey
cut, to	potong	aru-
daily	s'hari hari	nadorlum
damage	rosak	nasham
dance, to	m'nari	adu–
danger	bahia	abayam
dark	glap	karutha
date (day)	hari–bulan	nal
daughter	anak prempuan	magal
dawn	pagi–pagi	vidiyal
day	hari	nal
dead	mati	sha
dear (cost)	mahal	viley

BENGALI	RUSSIAN
ash–	pri'idti
bishoi	pri
baburchi	povar
rann– ; kor–	gatovit
kon	ug'l
t'ik	pravilni
dam	ts'na
tulo	khlop'k
gun–	s'chitat
desh	str'na
ut'an	dvor
d'ak–	pokrıvat
goru	korova
b'ir	t'lpa
bati ; peyala	chashka
almari	shkaf
porda	zan'vyes
balish	padushka
kat–	rezat
rojkar	yezh'dnyevni
k'hoti	ubit'k
nach kor–	tantsovat
bipod	apasnost
ond'okar	tyomni
tarikh	data
meye	doch
b'or–bela ; protush	z'rya
din	dyen
mora	myortvi
dami	dar'goi

ENGLISH	MALAY	TAMIL
deep	dalam	arlamana
die	mati	sha–
difficult	susa	prayasamana
dig	gali	kindu–
dinner	makanan	thini
dirty	kotor	alukulla
dish	ping–gan	pingan
district	negri ; desa	taluka
do	bikin ; bua'	shey–
don't !	jangan	–adeyyum
doctor	dukun ; doktor	vaithiyan; doktor
dog	anjing	nai
donkey	kaldai	kaludhey
door	pintu	kadhavu
down	bawa	kirley
drain, a	parit	kan
dress, a	pakaian	adey
drink, to	minum	kudi–
drive, to	jalang kreta	ottu–
drop (let fall)	jatohkan	kirley vidu–
duck	itek	vathu
dust	habok	thushi
each	masing masing	adhu-adhu
east	timor	kirl
easy	s'nang	leshana
eat	makan	un–
egg	t'lor	muttey
eight	d'lapan	ettu ; en
eleven	s'blas	padhin-onru
empty	kosong	verumeyana

BENGALI	RUSSIAN
gob'ir	gluboki
mor–	um'rat
shokto	trudni
k'ur–	k'pat
rater k'aoa	abyet
moila	gryazni
t'hala	blyudo
jela	okrug
kor–	dyel't
–o na !	nye
daktar	doktor
kukur	sabaka
gad'a	asyol
dorja	dver
niche	vnizu
nali	vad'stok
kapor ; sari	platye
pan kor– ; kha–	pit
chalan–	yekh't
phel–	r'nyat
hansh	utka
d'ulo	pil
protek	kazhdi
prabdik	v'stok
shahoj	lyogki
k'a–	yest
dim	yaitso
at	vosyem
egaro	adinatsat
k'ali	pustoi

ENGLISH	MALAY	TAMIL
end	hujong	mudivu
enemy	muso	virodhi
enough	chukop	podhum
enter	maso'	piraveyshi–
envelope	emblop	kadudashi urey
evening	p'tang	maley
explain	kasi tau	shol–
extinguish	bikin mati	iru–
extra	l'bey	micham
eye	mata	kan
face	muka	mugam
fall, to	jato	virlu–
family	isi ruma	kudumbam
fan	kipas	vishiri
far	jau	nediya
farmer	peladang	shamushari
fasten	ikat	puttu–
fat (stout)	g'mok	parutha
father	bapa	thandhey
fear, to	takot	payam
feast	makanan b'sar	virundu
feed, to	makan	mey–
female	prempuan	pen
fence	pagar	veyli
fetch	ambil	kondu va–
fever	d'mam	juram
few	s'dikit	shila
field	padang	vayal
fight, to	berklahi	shandey shey–
find, to	dapat	kandu pidi–

BENGALI	RUSSIAN
shesh ; k'atom	k'nyets
dushmon ; shotru	vrag
joteshto	davolno
d'uk–	vo'idti
k'am	kanvyairt
shond'e	vyecher
bujiye deo–	abyasnit
bond kor	g'sit
baki	sverkh
chok	glaz
muk'	litso
por–	pad't
sombond'	syemya
pak'a	vyair
dur	daly'ko
krishan ; chashi	krestyanin
bond–	privyaziv't
mota	tolsti
baba ; pita	atyets
boy kor– ; dor–	bayatsya
boro–din	prazdnik
ahar kor–	kormit
strilok	samka
bera	zag'rodka
an–	po'idti za
jor	likharadka
gota–kotok	nyemnoghie
mot'	polye
mar–	dratsya
paw–	nakh'dit

ENGLISH	MALAY	TAMIL
finger	jari	viral
finish	bikin habis	iru–
fire	api	anal
first	pertama	mudal
fish	lian	min
five	lima	anju
flag	b'ndera	kodi
flat	rata	thatteyana
flood	ayer ba	vellam
floor	lantai	thalam
flour	t'pong	ma
flower	bunga	pushpum
fly, a	lalat	i
fog	kabut	mashi
fold, to	lipat	madi
follow	ikut	pin shel–
food	makanan	thini
foot	kaki	adi
for (prep.)	bagi	–aga
foreigner	orang dagang	varli-pokkan
forest	utang	kadu
forget	lupa	mara–
fork	garfu	mul
fort	khota	kottey
four	ampat	nal ; nangu
friend	kawan	kuttali
from	deri	–il
front, in	di muka	munbu
fruit	bua	param
fry	goring	adu–
fuel	kayu api	viragu

BENGALI	RUSSIAN
angul	palyets
k'atom kor	konchit
agun	agon
poila	pyervi
mach	riba
panch	pyat
nishan	flag
chepta	ploski
joar	p'top
meje	pol
ata ; moida	tyesto
p'ul	tsvet'k
machi	mukha
koasha	tuman
noan	sgibat
pichu dor–	sledavat
k'abar–jinish	yeda
pa	n'ga
–jonno	dlya
ajnabi	in'stranets
jongol ; bon	lyes
bule ja–	z'bit
kanta	vilka
prashad	fort
char	ch'tire
bondu	drug
–hote	ot
–age	pyer'd
p'ol	plod
b'aj–	zaz'harivat
kat–koila	topl'vo

ENGLISH	MALAY	TAMIL
garden	k'bun	tottam
gate	pintu	totta wari
gather	kumpol	kuttu–
gentleman	tuan	thurey
get	dapat	vangu–
girl	anak prempuan	kanni
give	kasi ; bri	i–
glass (drinking)	glas	thambalar
glass (looking)	chermin muka	kannadi
glove	sarong tangan	keyurey
goat	kambing	kera
go	p'gi	shel–
good	bai'	nalla
goods	barang barang	shaman
god	allah	theyvan
gold	'mas	pon
government	saltanat	sharkkar
gown	pakaian	adey
grain	gandom	akkam
grass	rumput	pul
grave, a	kubur	pireydhak kurli
grease	minyak	korluppu
great	b'sar	periya
green	nijau	pashu
greet	kasi tabek	yettu-kol–
ground	tana	nilam
grow	tumbo	perugu–
guest	tamu	virundu
guide	pandu	varli–kattu–
gun	snapang	vedi thokku

BENGALI	RUSSIAN
bagan	sad
p'otok	dver
shongroho kor–	sob'rat
shaheb	g'sp'din
pao–	dabitsya
meye	dyev'shka
deo–	dat
g'lash	st'kan
arshi ; aina	z'rkalo
dostana	pyerchatka
chagol	k'za
jao–	idti
b'alo ; uttom	kh'roshi
mal	t'var
(porom–) ishor ; alla	bawg
shona	zol'to
sharkar	pravit'lstvo
poshak ; sari	platye
b'usa	zerno
g'ash	tr'va
gor ; kobor	yama
tel	salo
boro ; mohot	balshoi ; veliki
kancha ; anari	z'lyoni
nomoshkar deo–	pazdr'vlyat
mati	z'mlya
bar–	r'sti
bondu	gost
prodorshok	prav'dnik
bonduk	ruzhe

ENGLISH	MALAY	TAMIL
hair	bulu	mayir
half	s't'nga	arey
hand	tangan	kai
handkerchief	sapu tangan	lenji
handle	tangan	kai
happen	jadi	neyridu–
happy	suka hati	nalla
hat	topi	thoppi
he	dia ; ia	avan
head	k'pala	taley
hear	d'ngar	kel–
heart	hati	irduhayam
heaven	shorga	paralogam
heavy	brat	paramana
hedge	pagar	veyli
hen	ayam b'tina	pettey
here	sini	ingey
high	tingi	uyaramana
hill	bukit	maley
hire, to	sewa	vadageyku edu–
his	dia punya	avan ; aval
home	ruma	vidu
home, at	di ruma	vidu
honest	tulus	neyrana
honey	manisan leba	theyn
hope, to	harap	kathiru–
horse	kuda	kudhirey
hospital	ruma sakit	aspital
hot	panas	shudana
hotel	ruma tumpangan	hotel
hour	jam	mani

BENGALI	RUSSIAN
chul ; kesh	vol'si
ad	pal'vina
hat	r'ka
hat-chadar	nas'voi pl'tok
hat	ruchka
ho'o-	sluchatsya
shukhi	s'chastlivi
tupi	shlyapa
se ; tini	on
mat'a	gal'va
shun-	slish't
ridoi ; kolija	syertse
shorgo	nyebo
b'ari	ty'zholi
gacher bera	zabor
murgi	kuritsa
ek'ane	zdyes
unchu	visoki
pahar	kholm ; g'ra
b'ara kor-	nanimat
tar	yevo
g'ar	dom
barite	doma
shad'u	chestni
mod'u	myed
asha kor-	nady'yatsya
g'ora	losh'd
hashpatal	b'lnitsa
gorom ; topto	zharki
hotel	g'stin'tsa
g'onta	chas

ENGLISH	MALAY	TAMIL
house	ruma	vidu
how ?	b'gi-mana	yeppadi
how much ?	brapa	yevalavu
hundred, a	s'ratus	nuru
hunt, to	pembu–	kol–
hurt, to	luka	novup-paduthu–
husband	laki	purushan
hut	pondok	chinne vidu
I	saya	nan
if	kalau	anal
ill	sakit	viyadhiyula
immediately	skarang ini	udaney
important	brat	periya
ink	dawat ; tinta	mai
inn	pasangrahan	hotel
insect	binatang	i
interpreter	juru basa	thupashi
into	k'dalam	–ukku
iron	b'si	irumbu
is	ada	—
is not	tid'ada	alla
island	pulau	thivu
it	dia ; itu	adhu
jewel	permata	panidhi
journey	perjalanan	pirayanam
judge, a	hakim	nidhipadhi
jug	t'mpat ayer	kudam
jump, to	lompat	odu–
juice	ayer bua	yenney

BENGALI	RUSSIAN
bari	dom
kemon ; ki–kore	kak
koto	skolko
sho ; shoto	sto
shikar kor–	akhotitsya
koshto deo–	vredit
shami	muzh
kure ; kutir	izba
ami	ya
jodi	yesli
oshusto ; rogi	balnoi
tok'oni	seychas
aboshokio ; joruri	vazhni
kali	ch'rnila
shorai ; choti	kh'rchevnya
poka–makor	nas'kom'ye
dob'ashi	tolmach
–bitore ; –mod'e	v'
loha	zh'lyezo
(ache)	—
ney	nyet
dip	ostrof
ta	'no
gohona ; olonkar	drag'tsen'st
braman	p'yezdka
bicharpoti	sudya
kacher shorai	kruzhka
lapha–	skakat
rosha	sok

ENGLISH	MALAY	TAMIL
kettle	cherek	kettal
key	anak kunchi	shavi
kick, to	t'ndang	udhey–
kill	buno	kol–
kind (amiable)	berkasehan	kuttali
kind (sort)	macham	ach'u
king	raja	arashu
kitchen	dapur	kushini
knife	pisau	kathi
know, to	tau ; k'nal	ari–
lady	nonya ; mem	thurey-shani
lake	tasek	yeyri
lamb	anak domba	atuk–kutti
lamp	plita ; lampu	vilakku
land	tana	tharey
lane	lorong	aru
language	bahasa	pashey
large	b'sar	periya
last	akhir	mudivu
late	lambat	thamadham
laugh, to	tertawa	nagey–
law	undang-undang	shattam
lawyer	wakil	vakil
lead, to	impin	mudhi-ppo–
leaf	daun	iley
learn	blajar	padi–
leave (of absence)	hari l'pas	vidudhi
left (side)	kiri	idadhu
leg	kaki	kal

BENGALI	RUSSIAN
ketli	k'tyol
chabi	klyuch
pa mar–	udaryat
mere fel–	ubivat
d'ir	dobri
rup	rod
raja	k'rol
baburchi–kana	kukhnya
churi	nozh
jan–	znat
potni	dama
rod	oz'ro
berar bacha	b'rashek
bati ; alo	lampa
stol ; mati	z'mlya
goli	darozhka
basha	yazik
boro	balshoi
akhir	pasledni
haler	pozdni
hash–	smyeyatsya
ain	z'kon
ukil	adv'kat
pot–dekha–	vyesti
pata	list
shik–	uchitsya
ch'uti	atpusk
bam ; ba	lyevi
pa	n'ga

ENGLISH	MALAY	TAMIL
lend	pinjamkan	iraval kodu–
less	kurang	shattu
letter	surat	kagidham
lie down	baring	padu–
lift, to	angkat	thukku
light, a	trang	oli
light, to	rengan	chinne
light (weight)	pasang	anal
line	baris	nul
listen	d'ngar	kel–
little, a	s'dikit	shattu
live	tingal	shivi–
lock	kunchi	puttu
long (distance)	panjang	nediya
lose	hilang	irla–
love	kase'i	anbu
low	r'nda	kirley
madam	mem	amma
make	bua'; bikin	akku–
man	orang	manidhan
many	banya'	pala
map	p'ta	theysha–padam
market	pasar	karey teruö
marriage	kawin	kaliyanam
master	tuan	yeshaman
mat	tikar	pai
match	korek api	machis
mattress	tialm	methey
me	saya	yeney
meat	daging	mamisham

BENGALI	RUSSIAN
dar deo–	s'suzhat
kom	myenshe
chiti–kana	pismo
shue por–	lyeżhat
utan– ; tol–	padnimat
alo	svet
alo jal–	asvy'tit
halka	lyogki
shuta	linia
shon–	slushat
kom	nyemnogho
bach– ; bash kor–	zhit
kulup ; tala	z'mok
lomba	dlini
haran–	ty'ryat
balo bash–	lyubit
nicha	nizki
saheba	g'sp'zha
toiari kor–	dyel't
manush	muzhchina
bohu ; onek	mnogie
naksha	karta
bajar ; hat	rin'k
bie ; bibaho	brak
monib	kh'zain
galche	kovrik
diashlai	spichka
bichana	matras
amake	mnye
mansho	myaso

ENGLISH	MALAY	TAMIL
medicine	obat	marundhu
meet	jumpa	shandhi–
meeting	perkumpolan	kuttam
mend	m'mbaiki	parludhu par–
merchant	tukang berniaga	varthagan
midnight	t'nga malam	nadu rathiri
milk	susu	pal
minute	minit	nimisham
mistake	sala	pishagu
money	wang	panam
monkey	munyit	kurangu
month	bulan	masham
moon	bulan	nila
more	lagi ; lebi	miga
morning	pagi	kaley
mosque	masjid	masjid
most	paling	uththamam
mother	mak	amma
motor-car	kreta	gari ; motor
mountain	gunong	maley
mouth	mulut	wai
move, to	bergra'	irlu–
Mr.	tuan	yeshaman
Mrs.	mem	thurey–shani
much	banya'	miga
mud	lumpur	sheyru
mule	kaldai	karudhey
music	bunyi bunyian	shangidham
my	saya punya	yen
nail (iron)	paku	ani
name	nama	peyr

BENGALI	RUSSIAN
oshüd	myed'tsina
deka kor–	vstr'chat
saksat	vstrecha
meramot kor–	pach'nyat
bonik	kupyets
dupur–rat	poln'ch
dud ; kir	mal'ko
minit	minuta
bul	ashibka
taka	dyengi
banor	abyezyana
mash	myesy'ts
chand	l'na
aro onek ; boi	bolshe
shokal	utro
moshjid	musulmanski khram
beshi ; odikansho	sami
ma ; mata	mat
gari	mashina ; avt'm'bil
porbot	g'ra
muk	rot
nor– ; nora–	dv'gat
shaheb	g'sp'din
shaheba	g'sp'zha
onekta	mnogho
doba	gryaz
k'ochor	mul
bajna	musika
amar	moi ; maya
alpin	gvozd
nam	imya

ENGLISH	MALAY	TAMIL
narrow	s'mpet	melliya
nation	bangsa	shanam
near	d'kat	andheyil
nearly	hampir	konjang kureya
necessary	usa	periya
needle	jarom	ushi
never	ta'perna	oru kalum illey
new	b'aru	ila
news	khabar	sheydhi
newspaper	surat khabar	kagidham
next	k'mdian	andheyil
night	malam	ira
nine	s'mbilan	onbadhu
no	tida'	illey
noon	t'nga hari	mathiyanam
north	utara	vada
nose	hidong	mukkö
not	tida'	alla
nothing	tid'apa	onrum illey
now	skarang	ippo
number	angka	ilakkam
o'clock	pukol	mani
of	punya	–in
office	ofis	opis
officer	afsar	ofiser
often	banya' kali	adikkadi
oil	minyak	yenney
O.K. (all right)	baila	nalla
old	lama ; tua	parla
on	atas	–in meyl

BENGALI	RUSSIAN
shoru	uzki
jati	narod
kache	blizki
prai	p'chti
dorkari	nuzhni
chunch	igolka
kokono na	nik'ghda
notun ; nobo	novi
khobor ; shonbad	izvestia
akhbar	g'zyeta
porer	sleduy'shchi
rat	noch
noi	dyevy't
na	nyet
dupur	poldyen
uttor	syever
nak	nos
na	nye
kichu–na	nishto ; nish'vo
ek'on	t'pyer
somkya ; gonona	nom'r
bejeche	chas(of)
–er	—
apish ; doptor	k'ntora
ofsar	kam'ndir ; ofitser
prai ; kub	chasto
tel	maslo
ach'a	khar'sho
purano ; bura	stari
–upor(e)	na

ENGLISH	MALAY	TAMIL
once	s'kali	orutharam
one	satu ; sa	onnu ; or
only	sa'aja	mathiram
open	terbuka	thira
or	atau	alladhu
orange	jeruk manis	naranju
order, to	suro	katpi–
other	lain	para
our	kita punya	yen–gal
out	luar	thira
pack up	bungkuskan	adukku–
pain	sakit	no
paper	kertas	kagidham
path	jalan	aru
pay, to	bayer	i–
peace	damai	shamadhanam
pen	kalam	peney
pencil	patlut	pensil
people	orang-orang	shanam
pepper	lada	milagu
perfume	bau	moppam
person	s'orang	al
picture	gambar	shittiram
pig	babi	panni
pillow	bantal	thaleyaney
pin	pniti	ani
pineapple	nanas	anashi–parlam
pipe	panchuran	pili
place	t'mpat	thalam
plain (ground)	padang	maidanum

BENGALI	RUSSIAN
ek gun ; ek–bar	adin raz
ek	adin
k'ali	tolko
k'ol–	atkriti
kimba ; otoba	ili
komla–lebu	ap'lsin
ordar deo–; ajna	zak'zat
onno ; opor	drugoi
amader	nash'
ba'ire	vnye
jinish potro bad–	uklad'vat
koshto	mucheniye
kagoj	bumaga
(shoru) rasta	tr'pa
taka deo–	pl'tit
shanti	mir
kolom	py'ro
penshil	kar'ndash
lok	lyudi
morich	pyerets
pran	blago'khanie
bekti	litso ; chel'vyek
chobi	kartina
shuor	svinya
balish	padushka
alpin	bulavka
anarosh	ananas
nala	trubka
mati	myesto
shomotol bumi	ravnína

ENGLISH	MALAY	TAMIL
plant, a	poko'	nattu
plate	pingan	pingan
play, to	main–main	vileyadu–
pocket	kochek	shakku
poisonous	bisa	nanju
policeman	mata-mata	polisu
pond	tase'	yeyri
pony	kuda k'chil	kudhirey
porter	kuli	shumeykaren
possess	berole	pattu–
post office	post–ofis	tapal–opis
pot	blanga	kudam
potato	ubi b'ngala	uruley–kirlangu
pour, to	tuang	var–
prayer	minta do'a	shabam
present, to be	ada	ingey
price	herga	viley
priest	imam	kuru
prince	ana' raja	raja
prisoner	orang sala	kavalali
profession	jabat–an	uthiyogam
pull	tare'	irlu–
punish	hukumkan	thandi–
purse	pundi–pundi	panappey
put	taro	vai–
quarter	suku	kal
question	sual	kelvi
quick	l'kas	shikiramana
rabbit	—	mushal

BENGALI	RUSSIAN
udbid	rasteniye
shanok ; tala	taryelka
kela– ; baja–	igrat
poket ; jeb	k'rman
bisha	yadonosni
pahar–walla ; polis	militsy'ner
pukur	prud
tattu	poni
mute	nasilshchik
—	imyet
dak–g'ora	pachtovaya kantora
dekchi	gorshok
alu	kartoffel
dal–	vlivat
prartona	pros'ba
ro– ; tak–	bit
dam ; mullo ; bao	ts'na
guru	svyashchen'k
raja	prints
bondi	plyenik
kaj-korma	z'nyatiye
tan–	tyanut
shaja deo–	nakazivat
poishar toli	birzha
rak–	klast
shiki	chetvort
proshno	vapros
chotpote	skori
k'orgosh	krolik

ENGLISH	MALAY	TAMIL
rain	hujan	marley
raisins	bua angor	param
rat	tikus	yeli
railway	kreta api	rel
raw	b'aru	pachaiyana
razor	pisau chukor	shavara-katti
read, to	bacha	vashi–
ready	s'dia	thayar
receipt	r'sit	rashidhu
red	mera	shivapana
relation	saudara	inathar
remember	ingat	niṅeyvu kur–
remove	pinda	yeduthu
repair, to	baiki	parludhu par–
reply, to	jawab	shol–
rescue, to	l'paskan	iratchi
rest (repose)	perhentian	ileyparudhal
return (go back)	pulang	thirumbu–
rice (raw)	padi ; bras	nel
rice (cooked)	nasi	shoru
rich	kaya	periya
ride, to	tungang kuda	eyripo–
rifle	snapang	raiful
right (side)	kanan	valadhu
right (correct)	b'tul	niyayamana
ripe	masak	parlutha
rise, to	nai'	yerlu–
river	sungai	aru
road	jalan	teruö
roof	atap	modu
room	bile'	arey

BENGALI	RUSSIAN
brishti	dozhd
kishmish	izyum
boro idur	krisa
rel–pot	zh'leznya d'roga
taja	siroi
k'ur	britva
por–	ch'tat
toiari	g'tof
roshid	r'spiska
lal ; rokto	kraṣni
sombondo	rodstvyennik
mone kor–	pomnit
lo–	ud'lyat
meramotkor–	pach'nit
jobab deo–	atvyetit
bacha–	sp'sat
bisram	otdikh
p'ire ash–	vazvr'shchatsya
chal ; d'an	ris
b'at	ris
d'oni	b'gati
(g'ora) cho–	yekh't
bonduk	vintovka
dok'in ; dan	pravi
t'ik ; b'alo	pravilni
paka	spyeli
ut'– ; ot'–	padn'matsya
nodi	ry'ka
rasta ; shorok	d'roga
chal ; chat	krisha
kamra ; g'or	komn'ta

ENGLISH	MALAY	TAMIL
rope	tali (b'sar)	kayiru
rotten	burok	mel
rough	kasar	palmulla
rug	kajang	kambalam
run	lari	odu–
sack	karong	podhi
safe	s'lamat	pathiramana
salt	garam	uppu
same	sama	orey
sand	pasir	manal
sandals	trompa	sheruppu
sauce	kua	sawsu
savage	garang	kodiya
say	kata	shol–
scissors	gunting	kathirikol
school	skola	palikuram
screen	tembo'; tabir	shuvar
screw	p'ler itek	ani
sea	laut	kadal
seat	t'mpat dudok	ashanam
second	yang k'dua	irandavadhu
see	nampa'	kan–; par–
seek	chari	thedu–
sell	jual	vil–
send	kirim	anuppu–
seven	tujo	eru
several	b'brapa	pala ; anega
sew	jahit	thai–
shallow	tohor	arlam–atta
shave, to	chukor	shavaram

BENGALI	RUSSIAN
dori	v'ryovka
norom	gniloi
korkosh	grubi
galche	k'vyor
daura–	b'zhat
gant ; chot	m'shok
nirapod	byez'pasni
nun ; lobon	sol
eki ; shey	ad'nak'vi
bali	py'sok
k'orom ; chapli	sandalia
achar	sojus
nisht'ur	diki
bol–	sk'zat
kanchi	nozh'tsi
pat–shala ; iskul	shkola
porda	shirma
iskru	vintik
shomudro	more
boshbar jaiga	myest'
duir ; ditio	vt'roi
dek'–	sm'tret
k'onj–	iskat
bech– ; bikri kor–	pr'dat
pat'a–	p'slat
shat	syem
onek	nyeskolko
shelai kor–	shit
chotan	myelki
kama–	britsya

ENGLISH	MALAY	TAMIL
shawl	kain slendang	adey
sheep	domba ; kambing	kapal
she	dia ; bangsal	aval
sheet	slimut	duputi
ship	kapal	shimli ari
shirt	k'meja	kamis
shoe	kasut	chapat
shoot, to	temba'	kol–
shop	k'dai ; togo	karey
short	pende'	kittina
shoulder	bahu	thol
shout, to	bertria'	shatham podu–
show, to	tunjo'	kattu–
side	s'bla	akkam ; vila
sign	tanda	kurippu
sign, to	taro tanda tangan	kaiyoppam vai–
silk	sutra	pattu
silver	pera'	velli
since	sminja'	adhu–mudal
sir	tuan	aiya
sister	saudara prempuan	shagodhari
sit	dudo'	utkaru–
six	anam	aru
skin	kulit	uri
skirt	(kain) sarong	paware
sky	langit	vanam
sleep, to	tidor	urangu–
slow	lambat	thamadhamana
small	k'chil	chinne
smell, a	bau	moppam
smoke	asap	pugey

BENGALI	RUSSIAN
shal	shal
b'era	b'ran
tini ; se	'na
chador	pr'stinya
jahaj	k'rạbl
kamij	rubashka
juta	b'shmak
guli kor–	vistr'lit
dokan	mag'zin
choto ; k'ato	k'rotki
kand'	plecho
dak–	krichat
dek'a–	pak'zat
kank'	star'na
namer–polok	znak
shoi kor	padp'satsya
reshom	sholk
rupa	ser'bro
karon ; –hote	so vrem'ni kak
sahab ; babu ; mia	(g'sp'din)
bogini ; didi	sy'stra
bosh–	s'dyet
choi	shest
chamra	kozha
gagra ; shaya	yubka
akash	nyeb'
g'uma–	spat
d'ima–chal	myedl'ni
choto	mal'nki
pran	zap'kh
dumpan	dim

ENGLISH	MALAY	TAMIL
smoke, to	hisap roko'	pugey–kudi
snake	ular	pambu
snow	talji	–
so	b'gitu	appadi
soap	sabon	shavukaram
socks	sarong kaki	meyjoli
soft	l'mbot	mel
soil	tana	pumi
soldier	soldado	yuthashali
some	s'dikit	shila
something	satu barang	yeydho
sometimes	kadang kadang	adikkadi
son	ana' laki–laki	magan
song	lagu	pattu
soon	l'kas	shangidham
sorry	susa hati	vishanam
sort	jnis ; macham	achhu
soup	kua	suppu
sour	asam	pulipana
south	slatan	then
speak	chakap	peyshu–
spectacles	chermin mata	kannadi
spend	blanjakan	shelvarli–
spices	r'mpa–r'mpa	milagu
spoon	sudu	karandi
spring, a	mata ayer	uttu
stable	kandang	layam
stairs	tanga	thalam
stamp (postal)	s'tampa	thapal–muthirey
stand, to	berdiri	nil–
star	bintang	natshathiram

BENGALI	RUSSIAN
tamak khao	k'rit
shap	zmeya
borop ; tushar	snyeg
emon ; ey–rup	tak
shaban	milo
moja	n'ski
norom	myakhki
mati	z'mlya
shepai ; shoinik	s'ldat
(karao) ; kotok–ta	nyesk'lko
kichu	shto–n'but
kokono–kokono	in'khda
putro ; chele	sin
gan ; b'ajan	pyesnya
shiggir	skoro
duk'ito	zhal (–ushchi)
rup	sort
shurua ; sup	sup
tok	kisli
dok'in	yug
kota bol–	gav'rit
chashma	achki
koroch kor–	tratit
moshla	pryan'st
chamoch	lozhka
kuo	r'dnik
astabol	k'nyushnya
shinri	lyestn'tsa
ishtamp	marka
dara–	st'yat
tara	zvyezda

ENGLISH	MALAY	TAMIL
starch	kanji	korluppu
start, to	jalan	shel–
station, police	ruma pasong	polisu–opis
station, railway	s'teyshin	isteyshin
stay, to	nanti	iru–
steal	churi	thirludu–
steamer	kapal api	kappal
steel	baja	irumbu
stick	kayu	kambu
sting, a	s'ngat	kodukku
stocking	sarong kaki	meyjoli
stomach	prot	vayiru
stone	batu	kal
stop, to	tutop	nil–
storm	ribot	marley
story	chrita	kadhey
straight	lurus	neyrana
stranger	orang dagang	varli–pokkan
street	jalan	teruö
strike, to	pukol	arey–
string	tali	kayiru
strong	kua'	palmulla
study, to	blajar	padi–
sugar	gula	shini
summer	musim panas	kodey–kalam
sun	mata hari	shuriyan
supper	makanan	thini
swamp	paya	yeyri
swim	bernang	nindhu
table	meja	meyshey

BENGALI	RUSSIAN
mar	krakhmal
jatra kor–	nach'nat
t'ana	uchast'k
ishtishan	v'kzal ; stantsia
t'am–	ast'vatsya
churi kor–	krast
jahaj	par'khod
ishpat	stal
chori ; lat'i	palka
hul ; donshon	zhal'
moja	chulka
pakost'oli	zheludok
pat'or–	kamen
t'am–	ast'navl'vat
j'or	burya
uponesh	raskaz
shorol ; shoja	pryam'
jatri	in'stranets
rasta ; shorok	ul'tsa
mar–	bit
shuto	v'ryofka
boloban	silni
od'oyon kor–	iz'chat
chini	sakh'r
gormi (kal)	lyet'
shuji ; shurjo	solntse
rater khaoa	uzhin
j'il ; dig'i	b'lot'
shatra–	plav't
mej ; tebil	stol

ENGLISH	MALAY	TAMIL
tailor	tukang jahit	thaiyatkaran
take away	bawa p'gi	shumandhu po
take (hold of)	p'gang	pattu–
talk, to	chakap	shol–
tank (reservoir)	tase'	kulam
tea	ayer tey	they
teach	ajarkan	podhi–
teacher	guru	kuru
telegram	p'rkabran kawat	telegrammu
tell, to	bri tau	shol–
temple	kaba	kovil
ten	s'pulo	pathu
tent	k'ema	kudaram
than	deri pada	parkilum
that	itu	udhu
their	dia-orang	avar
then	k'mdian	anru
there	sana	angey
therefore	s'bab itu	adhalal
they	dia	avar
thick	t'bal	kattiyana
thief	p'nchuri	kallan
thin	nipis	melliya
thing	barang ; perkara	kariyam
think	fikir	shindhi–
this	ini	indha
thousand	s'ribu	ayiram
thread	b'nang	nul
three	tiga	mu (–nu)
throw, to	lempar	yeri–
ticket	tikit	shittu

BENGALI	RUSSIAN
dorji	p'rtnoi
lo–	vzyat ; snimat
grohon kor–	khvatat
kot'a ko–	gav'rit
puk'ur	rez'vwar
cha	chai
shikha–	uchit
shik'ok	uchit'l
telegram	telegrama
bol–	so'bshchat
mondir ; debaloi	khram
dosh	dyesy't
tombu	p'latka
–cheye	chyem
ki ; oi ; ota ; je	tot ; ta ; to
tader	ikh
tobe	t'khda
shekane ; sheta	tam
tai ; shey–hetu	poet'mu
tara	'ni
puru ; mota	tolsti
chur	vor
soru ; roga	kh'doi
kichu ; mal	vyeshch
chinta kor–	dum't
ey ; ini ; eta	et'
hajar	tisy'cha
shuta	nitka
tin	tri
chor–	br'sat
tikit	bilyet

ENGLISH	MALAY	TAMIL
tie, to	ikat	kattu–
time	waktu	kalam
tin	tima	thagaram
to	'k';pada	–ukku
today	ini hari	inru
together	sama sama	kuda
tomorrow	eso'	naley
tonight	ini malam	inru iravil
too (much)	terlalu	miga
tooth	gigi	pal
torch	sulo	thivatti
touch, to	jama	thodu–
towards	k' ; s'bla	–ukku
towel	tuala	tuwali
tower	k'ota	koburam
town	negri	pattanam
track	jalan	aru
trade, to	berniaga	viyabaram
trail (railway)	kreta api	rel ; gari
translate, to	salinkan k'basa lain	thiruppu–
travel, to	perjalan	payanam po–
traveller	orang dagang	varli–pokkan
tree	poko'	maram
tribe	bangsa	shanam
trousers	sluar	kalchattey
true	b'nar	meyyana
try, to	choba	piraishap padu–
turban	s'rban	taleypa
twelve	dua blas	pann–irandhu
twenty	dua pulo	iru–badhu

BENGALI	RUSSIAN
band–	zavy'zat
kal	vremya
tin	zhest
–prati ; –ke	k'
aj	sevodnya
ekotro	v'myeste
kal	zaftra
aj–rat	sevodnya nochu
boddo	slishkom
dant ; donto	zub
bati	svet
sporsho kor–	trog't
–prati ; –dike	p'napr'vleniyu
twale	pal'tentse
prashad	bashnya
shohor ; nogor	gor'd
(shoru) rasta	tr'pa
bikri kor–	torgovat
tren	poyezd
torjoma kor–	per'vod't
bromon kor–	put'shestv'vat
bromon–kari	put'shestv'nik
gach	dyer'va
jat	plemya
pajama ; pentulen	bryuki
shoto (–kar)	verni
cheshta kor–	prabovat
pogri	tyurban
baro	d'vnats't
bish ; kuri	dvats't

ENGLISH	MALAY	TAMIL
twice	dua kali	iru tharam
two	dua	iru
umbrella	payong	kudey
under	bawa	–in kirl
understand	tau ; m'ng'rti	ari–
uniform	sarupa	peydham iladha
up	atas	meyl
us	kita	yen–galey
useful	berguna	pirayoshanam–ulla
valley	l'mba ; paha'	maidanum
value	herga	viley
vegetables	sayur	kirey
veil	m'rgo'	mukkadu
very	banya'	miga
village	kampong	ur
visit, to	m'lawat	shandhi–
wages	gaji	shambalam
wait, to	nanti	kathiru–
wake, to	bangunkan	yerluppu–
walk, to	berjalan	nada–
wall	tembo'	shuvar
want, to	mau	theyveyai iru–
war	prang	yutham
warm	panas	anal–ulla
was	suda	–th– ; –nd–
wash, to	baso ; mandi	karluvu–
washerman	d'obi	wannan
watch (clock)	jam	kadiyaram

BENGALI	RUSSIAN
dui–bar	dvazhdi
dui ; du	dva
chati	zont
-niche	pod
buj–	p'nyat
wardi	mundir
uporer–dike	naverkh
amader	nam
kejo	polezni
upotoka	d'lina
dam ; bao	ts'na
shak–shobji	ov'shchi
orna ; g'omta	vual
k'ub ; besh	och'n
gram ; polli	d'ryevnya
mulakat kor–	pas'shchat
maine	plata
opek'a kor–	azh'dat
jaga–	budit
bera–	g'lyat
deyal	st'na
cha–	zh'lat
jang	voina
gorom ; topto	tyopli
chil–	bil (–o,–i)
dho–	mit
d'oba ; d'upi	prachka
tek–g'ari	chasi

ENGLISH	MALAY	TAMIL
watch, to	jaga	kavatka–
watchman	orang jaga	kavatkaran
water	ayer	tanir
water, drinking	ayer minum	kudika–tanir
way	jalan	varli ; aru
we	kita	nan–gal
weak	l'ma	pelavina
weapon	s'njata	ayudham
week	mingo	varam
were	suda	(–th– ; –nd–)
west	barat	meyl
wet	basa	iramana
what ?	apa	yenna
wheel	roda	rodhey
when ?	(apa) bila	yeppodhu
where ?	mana	yengey
which ?	yang mana	yedhu
white	putey	vel
who ?	siapa	ar
why ?	k'napa	yeyn
wide	lebar	agalamana
wife	bini	penshadhi
will (shall)	nanti ; mau ; buli	(–p– ; –b–)
wind (air)	angin	kattu
window	j'ndela	shannal
wine	angor	rasham
winter	musim dingin	kambi
wire	dawai	sharadu
with	d'ngan	–odu ; –udan
without	d'ngan tiada	–inri
woman	prempuan	manushi

BENGALI	RUSSIAN
pahara de–	nabl'dat
chokidar	storozh
jol	v'da
pan–jol	pit'vaya v'da
rasta	d'roga
amra	mi
durbol	slabi
jontro–pati	aruzhie
shoptaho ; hopta	n'dyelya
chil–	bili
poshchim	zap'd
b'ija	mokri
ki	shto
chokor	kal'so
kokon ; kobe	k'ghda
kon–kane	ghdye
ki ; ke	k'koi
shada	byeli
ke	kto
keno ; kijono	pach'mu
cho–ora	shiroki
stri ; potni	zh'na
–bo ; –ben	bud (–et, –ut)
hawa	vyet'r
janala	akno
mod	v'no
shit-kal	z'ma
tar	provoloka
–shonge	s'
–bagair	byez
strilok	zhenshch'na

ENGLISH	MALAY	TAMIL
wood	kayu	kambu
word	prekata'an	varthey
work (noun)	kerja	veyley
workman	tukang	veyleykaran
worse	kurang bai'	ketta
worship	s'mbayang	thorlu–
wound, a	luka	kayam
wrap up	bungkuskan	adukku
write	kulis	yerludu–
wrong	sala	ketta
year	tahun	andu
yellow	kuning	manjal
yes	ya	nalla
yesterday	s'malam ; k'lmarin	neyttu
you	angkau	nir
young	muda	ila
your	angkau (punya)	un

BENGALI	RUSSIAN
gach ; lakri	lyes ; deryevo
lafz	slov'
kaj	trud
mojur	rabochi
boddo k'arap	khuzhe
puja (kor–)	uvazhat
ag'at	yazva
jora–	svertivat
lek–	p'sat
b'ul ; onejo	ny'prav'lni
bochor	god
holde	zholti
ha	da ; tak
kal	vch'ra
apni ; apnara	vi
kochi ; torun	mal'doi
apnar	vash'

MALAY

Notes :

PRONUNCIATION : Words ending in k, t or an apostrophe are cut very short.

WORD ORDER : 'The' is omitted. 'A, an' is *sa* or *satu*. Adjectives follow nouns. 'Of' is often omitted ; thus 'the house of the headman' would be simply 'house : headman.'

PLURALS : Plurals are sometimes shown by doubling a noun ; thus, *orang* (man) : *orang–orang* (people). Where the context is clear, the plural is often not shown at all.

NUMERATIVE PARTICLES : When a noun follows a number, a particle (corresponding to 'piece' in the Pidgin English phrase 'one piece house') is used between number and noun. The commonest particles are :

alai	(generally used)	*butir*	(grain)
batang	(trunk)	*ekor*	(tail)
biji	(seed)	*kayu*	(stick)
bua	(fruit)	*orang*	(man, person)
		puchuk	(top)

Thus 'one mango' becomes *satu bua mangga.*

VERBS : Verbs do not change to show person, gender, number, etc. The simple form of the verb given in the lists is used for the present and for commands ; the past is shown by adding the word *suda* (was), the future by adding *mau* or *nanti* (will, shall). The passive is formed by prefixing *di–* to the verb. The prefixes *ber–* and *per–* form intransitive verbs, the suffixes *–kan* and *–i* give transitive forms.

MALAY

Special List :

aborigines . . .	orang-sakai ; orang-bukit
areca-nut . . .	pinang
attack (by a frenzied man)	(meng–) amok
bamboo . . .	bulu
banana . . .	pisang
betel-leaf . . .	sirih
blowpipe . . .	sumpit-an
Borneo . . .	brunei
cassowary . . .	kasuari
Ceram . . .	serang
chopping-knife . .	parang
civet	binturong
Cochin China . .	kuchi
cockatoo . . .	kakatuwa
curry . . .	lauk ; sambil
China . . .	benua china
dagger . . .	kris
devil	iblis ; jin
durian . . .	duren

England . . .	negri ingris
English . . .	ingris
Europe . . .	eropa
farewell . . .	s'lamat jalan
fish: (*Lates calcarifer*)	(ikan) kakap
fruit:	
(lime, lemon) . .	limau
(orange) . . .	limau manis
(large citrus) . .	pumpulmas
(pummelo) . .	,,
(jack-fruit) . .	chempadak
(coconut) . . .	klapa
gong	gong
gourd . . .	labu
grandfather (also used as a title) . . .	dato
guava	jambu
gutta-percha . .	percha ; geta-taban
greetings . . .	s'lamat ber-jumpa; tabek
grass, long . . .	lalang
house-lizard . .	chichak ; geko'
India . . .	benua k'ling
Indian . . .	(orang) k'ling
jacket	baju
Japan	negri jepun
Java(-nese) . . .	jawa
Malay . . .	(orang) malaiu

mango	(bua) mangga
mangosteen	(bua) manggis
mangrove	bakau; manggi-manggi
myna (bird)	(burong) tiong
mosquito	nyamok
mosquito net	klambu
palm-fronds (used as roofing)	atap
palm-leaves	kajang ; ola
papaya	betik
parrot	(burong) nuri
pomfret (fish)	(ikan) bawal
prawn	udang
rice-field	sawah ; bendang
roofing	atap
rubber	geta
sago	sagu
Siam	benua siam
skirt	(kain) sarong
Sumatra	pulau percha
tapir	tenok
thank you	trima kasi
tiger	harimau
weights: one lb. and one-third	kati
133lb. (100 *kati*)	pikul
wild tribes	orang-utan ; sakai ; semang
yam	ubi ache ; ubi gadong

TAMIL

Notes :

PRONUNCIATION : The first syllable is usually stressed.

WORD ORDER : Verbs come at the end of sentences, dependent clauses at the beginning. Adjectives precede nouns. 'The,' 'a,' and the forms of the verb 'to be' are usually omitted. Questions are indicated by *–a* being added to either the last or the stressed word in the sentence. Prepositions (more properly called postpositions) follow nouns ; *–in–* or *–ttu–* is often inserted between noun and postposition.

ENDINGS : Adjectives do not change, whatever their case or form. Nouns take a variety of case endings, which are given in the word-lists under the appropriate prepositions. Nouns in the accusative case take the ending *–ey* ; in the plural, the endings *–gal* or *–r* (the latter only when the noun denotes a person). Nouns ending in *–dhu* drop this ending in the plural and add *–nagal* or *–veygal.*

VERBS : The personal endings for verbs are :

I	you	he	she	it	we	they
–eyn	*–ir* (*gal*)	*–an*	*–al*	*–dhu,* *–ru, or* *–*(*k*)*um*	*–om*	*–arga*

Between these endings and the root of the verb, the

following links are placed to indicate tense:

–kir–	or	*–gir–* . .	present
–th–	or	*–nd–* . .	past
–p–	or	*–b–* . .	future

Imperative Forms:

rude . .	Root alone
mild . .	Root–*um*
polite . .	Root–*ungal*
negative . .	Root–*adey*–(*um* or *ungal*)

Other negative forms of the verbs are made by adding *–adhilley* after the tense and personal endings.

Word Forming: Adverbs are made from other words by adding *–ay* or *–aga.* Adjectives can often be used as roots for verbs. Other ways of forming new words are:

Noun – *ana* or *–agiya* ; this gives an adjective.
Noun – *ulla* ; this gives an adjective with the English ending '*–ful.*'
Noun – *atta* or *–ina* ; this gives an adjective with English ending '*–less.*'

The suffixes *–van*, *–karan*, *–ali* correspond to the English ending '*–man*' and can thus be used to form such words as 'boatman,' 'gardener,' etc.

TAMIL

Special List:

Arcot	arkad
accountant, recorder .	kanakan

Brahman . . .	namburi
cakes	apparu
Calicut . . .	kolikodu
carrying-yoke . .	kavadi
Cauvery River . .	kaveri
Cochin . . .	kochchi
coconut fibre . . .	kayiru
citron	nartey
Coleroon River . .	kolladam
commander (of troops) .	talavey
Comorin, Cape . .	kumari
Coorg	kodagu
Coromandel . . .	choromandalam
cow dung, dried and used as fuel . . .	varatti
curry	kari
Godavari . . .	godey
harvest festival . .	pongol
hire, wages . . .	kuli
jasmine	narum paney
jewel akin to sapphire .	kurundam
Jack-fruit . . .	sakkey
jhum (hillside cultivation abandoned after a few harvests) . . .	ponam
Konkan	konkanam
mango	mangey

master (*sahib*) . .	turai
mistress, ma'm . .	turaisani
millet (*jawar*) . . .	cholam
mongoose . . .	mangisu
mulligatawny . . .	milagu–tanir
Mysore . . .	maisur
Ootacamund . . .	ottagaimandu
patchouli . . .	pash'shilai
palm-leaf . . .	olai
pumpkin . . .	kumbalam
Pondicherry . . .	put'uvai ; put'usheri
raft . . .	katumaram
rest-house . . .	shattiram
rice, boiled . . .	muder
shed	pandal
teak	tekku
Tinnevelly . . .	tiru–nel–veli
Travancore . . .	tiruvankodu
trinket, worn by married women . . .	tali
Tuticorin . . .	tuttukkudi
wages	kuli
water in which rice has been boiled . . .	kanji

BENGALI

Notes :

WORD ORDER : The verb always goes to the end of a sentence. The verb ' to be ' in all its forms is usually omitted. Adjectives precede nouns. There is no equivalent for 'a', 'an' or 'the', but *ek* (one) is often used where in English ' a ' would precede a noun, and the suffix *–ta* or *–ti* (that) serves for ' the ' in many cases.

PLURALS : Nouns show the plural by adding *–ra* or *–gula* (*–ra* is chiefly used with nouns describing people). Adjectives do not change in the plural.

VERBS : Add the following endings to the roots given in the word-lists to form the various tenses, etc :

–(ch)i	1st person (I and we)	Present	(e.g. we eat)
–(ch)en	2nd and 3rd persons	,,	(e.g. they eat)
–ba,–bo	1st person	Future	(e.g. I will eat)
–ben	2nd and 3rd persons	,,	(e.g. you will eat)
–lam	1st person	Past	(e.g. we ate)
–len	2nd and 3rd persons	,,	(e.g. he, she ate)
–te	Present Participle (in this form the verb is usually said twice)		(e.g. eating).
–a	Passive Participle		(e.g. eaten)

FORMING WORDS : More words can be formed by adding the following suffixes to words in the word-lists :

–a	e.g.	*hat* (hand)	*hata* (sleeve)
–ai		*dal* (pour)	*dalai* (casting)
–ami, ma		*chele* (child)	*chelemi* (childishness)
–ar		*cham* (skin)	*chamar* (tanner)
–i		*desh* (country)	*deshi* (country-made)
		daka (Dacca)	*daka'i* (of Dacca)
–e		*nag'r* (town)	*nag're* (town-bred)
–o		*jol* (water)	*jolo* (watery)
–ola		*gari* (carriage)	*gariola* (driver)
–te		*b'ara* (rent)	*b'arate* (tenant; hired)
–ta, –twa		*nabin'* (fresh)	*nabin'ta* (freshness)

HAVE: There is no equivalent verb for 'have' in Bengali. 'The boy has a knife' is expressed by 'one knife is of the boy'; the Bengali order being 'boy–the–of one knife is' (*chele–ti–r ek churi ache*).

NUMERATIVE PARTICLES: When a number is used with a noun, a numerative particle (similar to the word 'piece' in the Pidgin English phrase 'one piece house') must be used. The commonest particles are:

–jan	for people
–ta	for things
–k'an	for flat things
–gach	for long thin things

Thus 'ten houses' is *dosh–k'an bari.*

BENGALI

Special List :

alligator	kumir
Arakanese, Chittagonian	mag
areca-nut . . .	shupari
art	lolito–kola
bamboo	bash'
Bengal	bangla–des
Bengali (person) . .	bangali
Bengali (adjective) . .	bangla
betel leaf . . .	pan
bison (*bos frontalis*) . .	gayal ; mit'an
boat, small . . .	dingi ; na
boat with roof . .	panshi
boatman	maji ; dari
brocade	kingkab
buffalo . . .	mosh
Calcutta	kolkata
chutney	chatni ; achar
corral used to trap elephants	keda
cultivation, often on mountain-side, in a jungle clearing which is abandoned after two or three harvests . . .	j'um
curds (*yaghourt*) . .	doi
curry	torkari ; kari

elephant . . .	hati
elephant, rogue . .	san
England . . .	ingland
English	imriji ; sahebi
European . . .	biliti
fig-tree (banyan) . .	bot-gach
fish :	
(*clupea ilisha*) . .	hilsa
(*lates calcarifer*) .	b'ikti
foods :	
mixture of curried vegetables	chechki
rice cooked with butter and pulses	kichuri
boiled meat and rice, with spices	polao
wheat wafers fried in *gi*	luchi
unleavened bread .	ruti
brinjal (*aubergine*) .	begun
France	fransa
fruits :	
Cape gooseberry .	tipari
custard-apple . .	ata ; nona
coconut . . .	narkol
jack-fruit . . .	kat'al
mango . . .	am
Germany . . .	jarmani
headman, landowner .	chaudri
Japan	japan

landing-stage	g'at
lizard	tiktiki
lotus	poddo
malaria	maleria
molasses	gur
mosquito	mosha
muslin	molmol
musician	kalwat
mystic	moromia
nationalist	shoraj–dola
opium	apim
pardon me	k'oma korben
parrot	tia
pepper, chilli	longka
prawn	bagda–chingri
painter	chitro-kor
please, (if you)	onugro'o kore
poet	kobi
procession	michil
puffed rice	muri
religion	dormo
rice-milk	payesh
rupee	taka
sacred place	tirtostan
saffron	jafran
scorpion	kakra–bicha
shrine	dorga

snake charmer . .	shapure
student	chatro
sweets	met'ai ; halua ; misti
(caseine sweet) . .	shondesh
(boiled sweet) . .	roshogolla
sweet potatoes . .	rangalu
take care ! . . .	shabd'an ! hushiar !
teak	shegun
thank you . . .	d'ono–bad
tiger	bag
turtle	kachim
university . . .	bisho–bideloi
vulture	shokuni
veranda	baranda
what's the matter ? . .	bepar ki ?
writer	lek'ok
warehouse . . .	gudam

Salutations :

To a Hindu . .	nomoshkar !
To a Moslem . .	selam !

Part Four

AN ANGLO-ASIATIC GLOSSARY

AN ANGLO-ASIATIC GLOSSARY

This list contains words which, although in common use among English speakers in Asia, do not correspond precisely to any word in the local languages concerned.

amah / ayah . .	nursemaid (Portuguese *ama*, *aia*).
atoll . .	group or ring of coral islands enclosing a shallow lagoon (Maldive *atolu* ; Singhalese *atul* (inside)).
baht (to sling the)	(to talk) a language (Hindustani *bat*).
bandana. .	handkerchief of bright colours, with white spots (Hindustani *bandhna* (fasten)).
basha . .	bamboo shed or hut (Bengali *bansh* (bamboo)).
bearer . .	personal servant or waiter (perhaps originally from palanquin-bearer).
beriberi . .	a disease due to causes similar to those which produce scurvy (Singhalese *beri*, (debility)).
betel-nut .	more accurately, areca-nut wrapped in a betel leaf smeared with lime (Malayalam *vettila* (simple-leaf)).
bobachi . .	a cook (Hindustani *bawarchi*).

bobachi-kana . a kitchen, generally separated from the house to which it belongs (Hindustani *bawarchi-khana*).

Bombay duck . dried *bummelo* fish.

bonze . . Buddhist priest (Japanese *bonzi*, *bonzo* (religious person) or *bo-zi* (teacher of the Law)).

bosh . . nonsense (Turkish *bosh* (empty)).

bottle-kana . pantry.

bo-tree . peepul-tree (Singhalese *bo*) or Indian fig-tree.

boxwalla . travelling pedlar or salesman.

boy . . servant.

Brahminy bull bull dedicated to Siva and turned loose in an Indian bazaar; or, more generally, Indian humped bull.

brain-fever bird Indian cuckoo with a maddeningly persistent cry.

brinjal . egg-plant (Portuguese *bringela*).

bummelo . a small fish (Mahratti *bombila*).

bund . . embankment, often with a road along the top; or a small bank dividing one rice-field from another (paddy-bund) (Hindustani *band*).

bunder-boat . small boat (Persian and Hindustani *bandar* (harbour)).

bungalow . European house (Hindustani *bangala* (Bengali)).

caddy . . small box for holding tea (Malay *kati* (one and one-third pounds weight)).

candy . . (sugar-candy)	crystallized sugar; sweets in general (Malayalam *kandi* (lump), Persian-Arabic *kand*).
cantonment .	military station or garrison town in India (archaic English word *canton* (to quarter soldiers)).
caste . .	hereditary class division among Hindus, based on common origin, occupation and inter-marriage (Portuguese *casta* (lineage)).
catty . .	a weight equal to one and one-third pounds (Malay *kati*).
chatty . .	earthen pot (Telugu *chatti*).
chawl . .	tenement house in an Indian slum quarter.
cheroot . .	cigar, generally with the ends cut off (Malayalam *churuttu* (a roll)).
Chetty . .	a Southern Indian merchant (Malayalam *chetti*).
chilli . .	dried pod of red pepper (Mexican *chilli*).
chin-chin .	cheerio, so long, goodbye, or good health (Pekingese *ching-ching* (thank you.)).
chit ; chitty .	voucher given instead of cash payment ; testimonial given to a servant, etc. (Hindustani *chitt'i* (letter)).
chokra ; chico	boy, servant-boy, urchin (Hindustani *ch'okra*).
chop . .	seal-impression, stamp or mark of authority (although now used

	mostly on the China coast and in the South Seas, this word comes from the Hindustani *ch'ap*).
chop-chop .	Pidgin English for 'be quick' (Cantonese *kap-kap*).
chopsticks .	pair of small sticks used to carry food to the mouth (in Chinese they are called 'quick things,' and the Cantonese *kap* (quick) is presumably the origin of 'chopsticks').
chukker .	a bout, or period, in polo and other games (Hindustani *chakkar* (circle)).
coir . .	coconut fibre (Malayalam *kayar* (cord)).
collector .	district administrative officer and magistrate in parts of India (a translation of the Moghul title of *tahsildar*, which comes from the Arabic *tahsil* (to collect)).
compound .	enclosure round a house, factory or group of buildings (perhaps from Malay *kampong* (village)).
compradore .	butler or steward (Portuguese *comprador* (purchaser)).
copra . .	dried kernel of the coconut, from which oil is extracted (Malayalam *kopparu*)
country-boat country-born country-made etc.	'country–' is used in India to indicate the local origin of many things and people. (translation of Hindustani *desi*).

crore . .	ten million (generally used of rupees) (Hindustani *karor*).
curry . .	spiced concoction of vegetables, fish, meat or eggs eaten with rice or unleavened bread (Tamil *kari*).
cutcha . .	crude, half-done (Hindustani *kach'a*). A 'cutcha' road is an unmetalled road; a 'cutcha' building is one of mud or crude brickwork; a 'cutcha' piece of work is a shoddily done one. 'Cutcha' is in every way the opposite of 'pukka.'
dacoit . .	robber belonging to an armed gang (Hindustani *dakait*, *daku*). Hence 'dacoity.'
dah . .	short sword or hacking-knife (Burmese *da*).
dandy . .	boatman; ascetic distinguished by carrying a staff; hammock slung from a pole carried by two or more men, used as a conveyance in hilly country (all from Hindustani and Bengali *dand* (staff, pole)).
dak-bungalow	rest-house maintained by the government (Hindustani *dak* mail, post)).
dengue . .	fever marked by pain in the joints (probably a Zanzibar word; not used in the East before 1860).
dhow, dow .	sailing vessel of Arab build (not an

Arabic word; possibly of Persian origin, through *dav* (run)).

dinghy . . small boat (Hindustani and Bengali *dingi*).

dixie . . cooking pot (Hindustani *degchi*).

dungarees . clothes of coarse calico (Hindustani *dungri*).

ghoul . . demon, generally inhabiting a wilderness (Arabic *ghul*, Persian *ghol*).

godown . warehouse (Singhalese *gudama*, Telugu *gidangi*).

gunny . sacking, sacks (Hindustani *goni*).

gymkhana . sports club or sports meeting (perhaps from Hindustani *gend-khana* (ballhouse) used of a rackets court).

howdah . seat carried on an elephant's back (Arabic *haudaj*, more properly used of camels).

hubble-bubble pipe in which a mixture of tobacco and spices is smoked through water.

jack-fruit . a huge and very sweet fruit (Malayalam *chakka*).

joss . image or idol (Portuguese *deos* (god)). Hence 'joss-house' (temple), 'joss-stick' (stick of incense).

juggernaut . (Sanskrit *jaganath*), a name under

which Krishna is worshipped in parts of India; also used of the massive carriage in which images of the god are drawn in public processions.

junk . .	Chinese sailing-ship (Javanese *jong* (large ship)).
khaki . .	dust-coloured (Hindustani *k'aki*).
kincob . .	gold brocade (Persian and Hindustani *kamk'ab*).
kukri . .	curved knife used by Gurkhas (Hindustani *kukri*).
kowtow	to touch the forehead to the ground in salutation (Chinese *ko-tau* (knock-head)).
koi-hai . .	a veteran British resident in eastern India (from Hindustani *koi hai* (anyone there?), a phrase used to call for servants).
lakh . .	100,000 (often rupees) (Hindustani *lak'*).
lascar . .	Asiatic (generally Indian) sailor. (Persian *lashkari* (a common soldier)).
mahout . .	elephant-driver (Hindustani *mahawat*).
mango . .	a soft and very sweet fruit (Tamil *mangey*).
mangosteen .	another sweet fruit (Malay *manggis* or *manggusta*).

mangrove .	dense growth found both above and below the water-line in tropical tidal estuaries (Malay *manggi-manggi*).
maskee . .	Pidgin English for 'never mind' (Portuguese *mas que* (in spite of)).
maund . .	weight varying from 28 to 82 lb. (Hindustani *man*; a word of great antiquity, cf. Arabic *mena*, Latin *mina*, Greek *m'na*, and the *m'na* or *men* found in Egyptian hieroglyphic inscriptions).
mem-sahib .	an English lady; Mrs. (English *ma'am*, Hindustani *sahib*). In Malaya *mem* alone is used in the same sense.
mofussil .	the countryside around an Indian city; up-country (Hindustani and Arabic *mufassal adalat* (a separate, i.e. provincial, court)).
monsoon .	the winds which bring the great yearly rains to the Far East; the rains themselves; or the time of great rains (Arabic *mausim* (season)).
mufti .	army slang for civilian clothes (Arabic *mufti* (an expounder of Moslem law); the connection is obscure. *Mufti* may originally have meant a loose dressing-gown which was perhaps thought to resemble a Moslem official robe).

mulligatawny .	peppery soup (Tamil *milagu-tanir* (pepper water)).
mongoose .	ferret-like animal (Telugu *man-gisu*).
muslin . .	cloth of fine texture, originally from Mosul (Mausil) in Iraq (Arabic *mausili*).
mussulman .	Muslim or Mahomedan (corruption from the plural forms of *muslim*, which are in Arabic *muslimin* and in Persian *musliman*).
must . .	frenzied; applied chiefly to elephants (Persian *mast* (drunk)).
nabob . .	corruption of Hindustani *nawab* (a governor, or a rank equivalent to a peerage); formerly used to describe Englishmen who returned home with fortunes made in the East.
nerrick rate .	standard rate for wages or prices, published by a local authority in India (Persian *nirkh*).
orang-utang .	great man-like ape (from Malay *orang-utan* (man of the forest); but in modern Malay *orang-utan* now means a jungle tribesman).
paddy-bird .	a kind of heron, usually white, which is commonly seen in rice-fields (Malay *padi* (rice)).

paddy-field .	rice-field, generally in its flooded state.
pagoda . .	temple or tower (possibly from Sanskrit *b'agavat* (holy, divine) through Portuguese *pagode*).
palanquin .	travelling litter carried by several men (Portuguese *palanquin* from Malay *palangki*, Telugu *pallaki*).
pariah . .	outcaste (Tamil *paraiyar*, a low caste very numerous around Madras ;' not used by Tamil speakers to describe outcastes).
pariah-dog or pie-dog	ownerless, generally mongrel, dog.
patchouli .	leaves of a plant akin to mint ; used as hair-scent, or as an ingredient in smoking tobacco. (Tamil *pash 'shilai*).
peon . .	messenger, orderly (Portuguese *peoa*).
pidgin . .	corruption of ' business.' Pidgin English is a jargon developed on the China coast between Englishmen and Chinese when neither understood the other's language. The grammar was largely based on Chinese, the vocabulary on English.
puggled .	crazy, foolish (Hindustani *pagal*).
polo . .	form of mounted hockey (*polo*, in the Balti dialect found in the

western Himalayas, means a polo-ball); played throughout Asia for centuries, and adopted by the English in Manipur in 1854.

pommelo or pummelo . large citrus fruit (Malay *pumpulmas*).

pukka . . ripe, well-built, genuine (Hindustani *pakka*); the opposite of *cutcha* (q.v.).

pug . . spoor, track of a wild animal (Hindustani *pag* (foot)). Hence *pagi*, a tracker.

punch . . drink composed of wine or spirits mixed with hot water, sugar, lemon, and spices (Hindustani *panch* (five); the constituents being usually five in number).

ryot . . peasant (Arabic *raiyat*, a collective term for 'subjects').

sago . . starch used as food, extracted from pith of a kind of palm (Malay *sagu*),

satin . . kind of silk cloth (from *Zaitun*, ancient port on the China coast, through Arabic *zaitunia*).

secunny . steersman or quartermaster (Persian *sukkani*).

seer . . weight approximately equal to 2 lb. (Hindustani *ser*).

sepoy . . Indian soldier (Hindustani and Persian *sipahi*).

serang . . skipper or chief hand on a small

native vessel (Hindustani and Persian *sar'ang* (commander)).

shagreen . . leather with granulated surface (Turkish and Persian *saghri*, meaning both the rump of a horse and the special leather originally only made from rumps).

shaman . . exorciser, devil-dancer (Tunguz *shaman*). Hence 'shamanism.'

shampoo . originally used to describe massage (from imperative of Hindustani *champna*, to press).

shroff . . money-changer; man employed to check the quality of coins; to sort coins (Arabic *sarraf*).

squeeze . . an illegal exaction.

sudder . . principal, main (Arabic *sadr*). Used in such phrases as 'sudder bazaar.'

suttee . . the rite of widow-burning (Sanskrit *sati*, a true woman).

syce . . groom; chauffeur (Hindustani and Arabic *sais*).

tamarind . (tree bearing a) fruit from whose pulp a drink is made (Persian *tamar-i-Hindi*, i.e. Indian date).

tank . . reservoir; artificial pond or lake. (Portuguese *tanque*, cf. French *étang*).

tat . . pony (Hindustani *tattu*).

teapoy . . small tripod table (Hindustani *tin pae* (three feet)).

terai hat. .	felt hat with broad brim and double thickness (from Hindustani *tarai*, damp country; particularly the humid belt of jungle country just south of the Himalayas).
thug . .	formerly one of a gang of robbers noted for strangling their victims (Hindustani *t'ag* (a swindler).
tical . .	a weight of silver; in Siam, a silver coin (Hindustani *t'ka*, Talaing *t'ke*).
ticca (gharry) .	hired (carriage) (Hindustani *t'ika* (hire)).
tiffin . .	lunch (from obsolete English *tiffing*, i.e. taking a snack between meals).
tindal . .	petty officer in a lascar crew (Malayalam *tandal*); foreman of a gang of labourers.
toddy . .	palm-wine, fermented from the sap of the palmyra, date, or coco-palm (Hindustani *tari*); hence, any hot sweetened drink.
tom-tom .	drum (Malay *ton-ton*, Tamil *tambattam*).
typhoon .	sudden storm, hurricane (Arabic, Persian and Hindustani *tufan*; Chinese *tai fung* (great wind)).
tycoon . .	powerful man; originally applied to the Japanese *shoguns* (Japanese *taikun* (great prince)).

veranda .	open gallery round or in front of a house (Bengali *baranda*, Sanskrit *varanda*).
viss . .	a weight equal to about 3 lb. (Tamil *visai* (division)).

Part Five

ASIATIC SCRIPTS

1. ARABIC (USED FOR TURKISH, ARABIC, PERSIAN, HINDUSTANI (URDU), AND MALAY).
2. NAGRI (USED FOR HINDUSTANI).
3. TAMIL.
4. BENGALI.
5. BURMESE.
6. SIAMESE.
7. CHINESE (USED FOR ALL CHINESE LANGUAGES AND FOR JAPANESE).
8. KANA (USED FOR JAPANESE).
9. RUSSIAN.

I. ARABIC

Used for Turkish (roman script is also used in Turkey), Arabic, Persian, Hindustani (Urdu), and Malay. The letters marked * are not used in Arabic itself. Arabic is written from right to left.

The final forms of Arabic letters resemble the isolated forms : medial forms resemble initial forms.

Isolated.	*Initial*		*Isolated.*	*Initial*	
ا		*a*	ظ	ظـ	*dh*
ب	بـ	*b*	ع	عـ	'
ت	تـ	*t*	غ	غـ	*gh*
ث	ثـ	*th*	ڠ	ڠـ	*ng**
ج	جـ	*j*	ف	فـ	*f*
چ	چـ	*ch**	ڤ	ڤـ	*p**
ح	حـ	*h*	ق	قـ	*q*
خ	خـ	*kh*	ک	کـ	*k*
د		*d**	ڭ	ڭـ	*g**
ذ		*dh*	ل	لـ	*l*
ر		*r*	م	مـ	*m*
ز		*z*	ن	نـ	*n*
س	سـ	*s*	و		*u, w*
ش	شـ	*sh*	ه	هـ	*h*
ص	صـ	*s*	ي	يـ	*i, y*
ض	ضـ	*dh, d*	پ	پـ	*ny**
ط	طـ	*t*			

2. NAGRI, HINDI, OR SANSKRIT

Used (mainly by Hindus) for Hindustani (Urdu). The letters in each word are joined together by the horizontal bar.

Vowels :—

अ	आ	इ	ई	उ	ऊ	ए	ऐ	ओ	औ
ă,'	*a*	*i*	*i*	*u*	*u*	*e*	*ey*	*o*	*au*

Consonants :—

क	च	ट	त	प
k	*ch*	*t*	*t*	*p*
ख	छ	ठ	थ	फ
k'	*ch'*	*t'*	*t'*	*p'*
ग	ज	ड	द	ब
g	*j*	*d*	*d*	*b*
घ	झ	ढ	ध	भ
g'	*j'*	*d'*	*d'*	*b'*
क़	ज़	ड़	न	म
q	*z*	*d, r*	*n*	*m*
ख़	श	र	स	फ़
kh	*sh*	*r*	*s*	*f*
ह	य	ग़	ल	व
h	*y*	*gh*	*l*	*v*

3. TAMIL

The second column gives the forms in which vowels are most commonly found, i.e. when combined with consonants.

க்	*k*	க	*k*
ங்	*ng*	கா	*ka*
ச்	*ch*	கி	*ki*
ஞ்	*ny*	கீ	*ki*
ட்	*d, t*	கு	*ku*
ண்	*n*	கூ	*ku*
த்	*th, dh*	கெ	*ke*
ந்	*n*	கே	*key*
ப்	*p, b*	கை	*kai*
ம்	*m*	கொ	*ko*
ய்	*y*	கோ	*ko*
ர்	*r*	கௌ	*kau*
ல்	*l*		
வ்	*v*		
ழ்	*l, zh*		
ள்	*l*		
ற்	*r, t*		
ன்	*n, nd*		

4. BENGALI

The forms shown are the simplest. Any two or three Bengali consonants can be combined to make a compound letter. The form of vowels varies according to the vowel's position in a word—initial, medial, or final.

ক	*k*	ল	*l*
ঘ	*g'*	ষ	*s ; sh*
চ	*ch*	হ	*h*
ছ	*ch'*	ড়	*r*
জ	*j*	ঢ়	*rh*
ড	*d*	ক্ষ	*k'*
ঢ	*d'*	গ	*g*
ত	*t*	ঙ	*ng*
দ	*d*	ঝ	*j'*
ন	*n*	ঞ	*n*
ফ	*f ; p'*	ঠ	*t'*
ব	*b*	ণ	*n*
ভ	*b'*	থ	*t'*
ম	*m*	ধ	*d*
য	*j ; y*	প	*p*
র	*rr*	শ	*sh*

5. BURMESE

Forms given for vowels are initial ones. When a vowel follows a consonant, the symbol အ is omitted and the consonant fills its place.

ဝ	*w*	ယ	*y*
ဓ	*d'*	လ	*l*
ဋ	*t, z*	က	*k*
ဈ	*z*	သ	*th*
ပ	*p*	ဘ	*b, p*
မ	*m*	ည	*ny*
ဖ	*p, b*	ဆ	*s*
ဗ	*b*	အာ	*a*
င	*n, ng*	အဲ	*e*
ဇ	*z*	အိ	*i*
ဠ	*l*	အီ	*i*
ခ	*ch*	အို	*o*
ရ	*y*	အု	*u*
ဒ	*d*	အူ	*u*
န	*n*	အော	*au*
ထ	*t'*	အော်	*aw*
တ	*t*	ေ	*ey*
ဟ	*h*		

6. SIAMESE

ก	*k*	ธ	*t'*
ข	*k'*	น	*n*
ฃ	*k'*	บ	*b*
ค	*k'*	ป	*p*
ฅ	*k'*	ผ	*p'*
ฆ	*k'*	ฝ	*f*
ง	*ng*	พ	*p'*
จ	*ch*	ฟ	*f*
ฉ	*ch*	ภ	*p'*
ช	*ch*	ม	*m*
ซ	*s*	ย	*y*
ฌ	*ch*	ร	*r*
ญ	*y*	ล	*l*
ฎ	*d, t*	ว	*w*
ฏ	*t*	ศ	*s*
ด	*d*	ษ	*s*
ต	*t*	ห	*h*
ถ	*t'*	อ	indicates a vowel
ท	*t'*		

7. CHINESE

Used for all Chinese dialects and sometimes for Japanese (in combination with Kana).

Normally characters are written in vertical columns. It is of course, only possible to give a few of the simplest and most useful characters.

人	person	日	sun; day
男	male; men	月	moon; month
女	female; women	山	mountain
入口	entrance	水	water
出口	exit	火	fire
注意	be careful	田	land; paddy-field
止	stop	皿	dish; plate
危險	danger	禾	rice (grain)
大	big; great	米	rice (polished); America
小	small; young	竹	bamboo

一	二	三	四	五	六	七	八	九	十
1	2	3	4	5	6	7	8	9	10

8. KANA

Used for Japanese (sometimes in combination with Chinese characters).

	Katakana		Hiragana
a	ア		あ
i	イ		い
u	ウ		う
e	エ		え
o	オ		お
ka	カ		か
ki	キ		き
ku	ク		く
ke	ケ		け
ko	コ		こ
sa	サ		さ
shi	シ		し
su	ス		す
se	セ		せ
so	ソ		そ
ta	タ		た
chi	チ		ち
tsu	ツ		つ
te	テ		て
to	ト		と
na	ナ		な
ni	ニ		に
nu	ヌ		ぬ
ne	ネ	子	ね
no			の

	Katakana		Hiragana
ha	ハ		は
hi	ヒ		ひ
fu	フ		ふ
he	ヘ		へ
ho	ホ		ほ
ma	マ		ま
mi	ミ		み
mu	ム		む
me	メ		め
mo	モ		も
ya	ヤ		や
yu	ユ		ゆ
yo	ヨ		よ
ra	ラ		ら
ri	リ		り
ru	ル		る
re	レ		れ
ro	ロ		ろ
wa	ワ		わ
(w)i	ヰ	井	ゐ
(w)e	ヱ		ゑ
(w)o	ヲ		を
n	ン		ん
v	ヴ		

9. RUSSIAN

Capital	Small	Transliteration
А	а	*a* (Italian)
Б	б	*b*
Д	д	*d*
Э	э	*e*
Е	е	*ye* (as in *yes*)
Ф	ф	*f*
Г	г	*g*
Ы	ы	*i* (in " is ")
И	и	*i* (in " machine ")
Й	й	*y* (in " boy ", " grey " etc.)
К	к	*k*
Л	л	*l*
М	м	*m*
Н	н	*n*
О	о	*o*
Ё	ё	*yo* (as in " yoke ")
П	п	*p*
Р	р	*r*
С	с	*s*
Т	т	*t*
У	у	*u* (in " put ")
Ю	ю	*yu* (as " you ")
В	в	*v*
З	з	*z*
Х	х	*kh* (as *ch* in *loch*)
Ц	ц	*ts*
Ч	ч	*ch*
Ш	ш	*sh*
Щ	щ	*shch*
Ж	ж	*zh*
Я	я	*ya* (as in *Yarrow*)
Ь	ь	*y* (as in *yes*, *young*, etc.)